SIRENS

Unpacking Painful Past Experiences to Lead Us to
Better Relationships, Communication, and Healing

by

CATHERINE BROOKS

©2024 by Catherine Brooks

Published by hope*books
2217 Matthews Township Pkwy
Suite D302
Matthews, NC 28105
www.hopebooks.com

hope*books is a division of hope*media

Printed in the United States of America

First paperback edition.

Paperback ISBN: 979-8-89185-209-9
Hardcover ISBN: 979-8-89185-131-3
Ebook ISBN: 979-8-89185-132-0
Library of Congress Number: 2024948136

hope*books
hopebooks.com
*Because the world needs your hope-filled
words now more than ever*

"Catherine has mastered the art of storytelling as a means to understand and heal from our own traumas and past. Each story engages, inspires, and gently challenges us to examine our lives while providing resources and an outlet to help us process them. I've never read a book on trauma quite like this. It's a unique breath of fresh air!"

Dr. Alex Swenson-Ridley DC, NBC-HWC, AMP
Mental Health, Wellbeing & Leadership Coach
Founder & Lady in Charge
Emergent Humans Center for Emotional Healing

"Catherine's insight and writings allow us to reflect deeper into our own experiences and explore healing in dynamic ways. Trauma and complex experiences can reverberate for generations. Having dynamic and accessible ways to access healing are important."

Dr. Allison Kelliher, MD
Associate Faculty for Indigenous Knowledges
and Practice Systems
Sr. Research Associate
John Hopkins School of Nursing and Bloomberg
School of Public Health Center for Indigenous Health

"*Sirens* is a powerful and compassionate guide for navigating the alarms our bodies send during times of stress and trauma. Through deeply personal stories, Catherine Brooks shares her experiences facing overwhelming challenges, as a teenager, young mother and wife and how they impacted her. Her vulnerability and practical insights provide readers with the tools to listen to their body's alarms, address the root causes of stress, and seek the support they need to begin the journey toward healing. This book is an essential resource for anyone ready to stop ignoring their body's warnings and embrace self-compassion and healing."

Kate Bartley, PT
CEO, She Walks in Wellness, Life Transformation &
Empowerment Coach

"Are you trying to heal from trauma, and looking for victory stories from someone who has healed? Catherine Brooks has faced much trauma in her life, and through this book, she gives you practical ways to heal from your traumas. You'll find compassion and wisdom through her stories of perseverance in trials, and you'll be affirmed and encouraged by her faith applications."

Sarah Geringer
Creative coach, book launch manager, editor, artist,
and author of seven books, including
Hope for the Hard Days:100 Encouraging Devotions

For Ramy

*Thank you for trusting me with your heart and never giving up,
even when it got hard - really hard.*

**For Abby, Molly & Zach, Wyatt, Sophia, Leah, Landon, and
those to come**

*You each hold pieces of my heart. May you benefit from my stories
and have better relationships, communication, and healing.*

For Emma and Jo

No one knows you like a sister.

**For all the people willing to work on the past today so that they
may have a better tomorrow**

May this book help bring you hope.

READER, PLEASE BE ADVISED

Chapter One contains descriptions of alcoholism and emotional child abuse.

Chapter Two contains descriptions of an accident, hospitalization, and traumatic loss.

Chapter Three contains descriptions of natural disasters, and violent human and animal deaths.

Chapter Four contains descriptions of depression and miscarriage.

Chapter Five contains descriptions of domestic violence, threats, gun use, and animal death.

Chapter Six contains descriptions of second trimester miscarriage.

Chapter Seven contains descriptions of a traumatic experience and forced counseling.

Chapter Eight contains descriptions of a traumatic death and loss.

Chapter Nine contains descriptions of diet culture, disordered eating, and general addiction practices.

CONTENTS

Chapter 1

THE WHY

As a child, I would excitedly race through stories, wanting to get to the happily-ever-after ending. As my exposure to the world grew, so did my realization that not every story had a happy ending. My life has certainly been filled with chapters that ended in sadness, but I have witnessed the transformative power of addressing our past so that we can experience peace.

It is important that I state that although I have some education, I am not a psychologist or trained therapist. I have read, listened to, and studied various topics over the years, but what you find in this book is from lived experiences. By no means do I have it all figured out. This book covers various topics, and each could be a book in and of itself. In fact, my original book proposal covered only one of the topics in the book. When I met with the director of publishing, she asked me questions about my life and challenged me to consider the "why" behind my book. As I contemplated her challenge, I had a conversation later that same day with a twenty-something who wanted advice on dealing with a tragedy. As we were ending our conversation, she asked me, "How do you know so much about how to respond to such challenging situations?" I responded, "Life has been doling out lessons for me since I was a little girl."

I found it easier to share my stories or lessons in one-on-one conversations as I could gauge my audience, knowing how much to share and which parts to leave out. I could acknowledge their situations and let them know I was not trying to compare my tragedy to theirs. I have been afraid to put the stories on paper because I have this ongoing dialog in my head that my trauma, challenges, or issues were "not as bad as someone else's," and I should just be thankful that things weren't worse. Although I believe being thankful creates a healthy perspective for us, in cases where we use it to be dismissive, it might not be helpful in moving us toward healing.

In Dr. Bruce Perry and Oprah Winfrey's book, *What Happened to You? Conversations on Trauma, Resilience, and Healing*, they discuss the challenge of defining trauma and how the word can be misused. One situation or event could be a trauma for one individual but build resilience for another. When defining trauma from a clinical standpoint, they consider the event, experience, and effects in an attempt to examine all the factors. The mental, physical, and social aspects all need to be considered when addressing trauma. All the pieces make everyone's experience unique, so comparison doesn't help.[1] Like the classic iceberg rising from the ocean, what we see in someone's life is only a tiny fraction of what may lie beneath the surface. I have attempted to use the word trauma carefully, but ask for grace if you find the word out of place in the book.

In this book, I examine the stories of my past that might help you recognize the benefit of dealing with traumatic or painful situations so you can have better relationships, communication, and healing. I found myself looking through notes, old journals, articles, and pieces of my past that I had taken the time to write down. Writing had been my escape. Writing has allowed me to see things I otherwise would not have recognized in my thoughts, feelings, and actions. I only wish I had been more consistent with my journaling. However, I did notice a trend in my writing. I often wrote when I was hurting, angry, or trying to figure something out. I naturally explored my thoughts and feelings through journaling. It makes sense why this was the case in light of neuroscience discoveries.

The act of handwriting involves a network of brain structures. Handwriting activates the motor cortex as well as the visual cortex to see the letters in our minds. Writing also consists of the language network that includes the central and temporal lobes. The complex web that handwriting sparks in our brain can create or make us aware of subconscious thoughts by bringing them to the surface and can have similar effects on the mind as meditation.[2] A study in 2012 and January 2024 highlights the benefits of handwriting over typing or keyboarding, explaining that handwriting fires more parts of our brain, increasing our brain connectivity.[3&4] The neuroscience field is fascinating, and we have only scratched the surface of understanding it. Although science and research can expand how we think about the topic of writing, I believe the testimonies of what writing one's story down does for a person also make a difference.

I must pause here to acknowledge that handwriting is a newer tradition and skill for some cultures, while oral skills and traditions may be more strongly developed and established. When we speak, we use both the temporal and frontal cortex. Although I still believe in the power of the pen, for some people, talking about their past with a trusted person or professional may be more effective for them. One technique shared in numerous books and articles is the empty-chair conversation, where one visualizes the individual that has hurt them sitting in the chair, and the person hurt says all the things they wished they could speak to the other person. Once you have said the words, you can decide what you want to do next. You will likely have a wave of emotions hit and need to sort through thoughts and feelings that surfaced during that experience. I encourage you to seek professional help to sort through the emotions if they seem overwhelming.

I suspect that, for most of us, a combination of writing and talking about events and experiences unlocks the effects they have on us. It is not about a technique being right or wrong but about finding something that helps you process the past – or at least pieces of your past – that can help you live a better present to create a brighter future. As I contemplated my thoughts on communication and processing thoughts, I realized my strong conviction regarding handwriting came from watching my husband write his childhood story for the first time in his early thirties. Although I had been writing in my journals for years and married for seven years, I had never considered the impact of writing on emotions and healing until I witnessed its impact.

We lived in a small cabin with our two little girls, nestled in the foothills of Denali National Park, where we cared for our 75 sled dogs. My husband ran races with the dogs, and we built a life around that lifestyle. Sled dogs had been a part of his life since childhood. During a work trip to Anchorage, Alaska, he met with a childhood acquaintance who happened to be involved with sponsorships. During the conversation, they spoke about some of their childhood memories. The friend challenged my husband to write his story. I knew pieces of his story, but I never envisioned what writing it down would put him through.

Our cabin was tiny, so my husband sat on the edge of the little kitchen with our family computer, attempting to put his memories to paper. At times, his fingers would strike the keys so hard that I was afraid the keyboard might break. Other times, I could see emotions building as low groans came from where he was writing. At one point, he jumped back from the computer, the chair hitting the wall as he flew out the door, anger and tears mixing as a deep roar came out. The girls and I were stunned into silence, unsure of what to do. I remember running to the door to ask if he was alright, only to be told he needed to be alone. My mind was racing with questions and concern – what had caused this sudden burst of emotion? He later reappeared and simply said, "This is harder than I thought it would be." He was reliving parts of his past that he had stuffed down inside.

He worked on the story for a few days. While he wrote, he was transported back in time, and our daughters and I were unsure where our husband and father had gone. He seemed distant, yet he needed to share things too. Sometimes, he would randomly start sharing a memory with us. I wish I would have had more mental health tools in my toolbox back then. I didn't know to ask him if he wanted me to help him with suggestions or just be a listener. To be honest, the story shocked me. My upbringing felt like a world away from his. I hope he understood how much I admired his strength and resilience. I also realized how, despite his ability to be a functional adult and love us, he had a lot of work to do.

Writing the story was the beginning of a healing journey. The story served as a platform to give us words and context to discuss difficult topics. Initially, the discussions could be like traversing a landmine, not knowing if a certain topic would trigger a hurtful memory, but as his partner, it gave me more understanding. I had to be careful not to weaponize the story or use it for pity, a concept I am not sure I initially understood.

Writing his story brought the darkness to the light. He met with his mom and sister and read his words to them. They shed tears and shared hugs. His mom expressed concern about whether the story should be shared with others. The purpose of sharing the story was and still is not about hurting others, but if sharing his story helps someone else have the courage to share theirs or get help, it was worth it. His sister courageously responded, "He is telling *his* story. It is his to share."

We now acknowledge and recognize that generational trauma had a crucial role to play in his childhood story. Colonization and boarding schools played a significant role in alcoholism as adults tried to numb the memories and pain. The Trans-Alaska pipeline brought massive change to the interior of Alaska and, for several years of construction, brought massive amounts of drugs and alcohol due to the influx of money and people.

What follows next is a short excerpt from my husband's story. His story covers many topics, tragedies, and sadness, but I have chosen a short selection as an example of using writing to process your story. I hope sharing this example will encourage you to begin to write your story. Your story might only cover a specific event, not a childhood. Whatever the story, know that writing or sharing it can be the first step in learning from our past for better relationships, communication, and healing. For my husband, writing his story was the beginning of healing. He is still on this journey.

The boy doesn't remember when he first noticed the drinking. That first winter, he was probably too young to notice, but one of his first memories is the night a man came along and took a bottle of gas that was on the porch in a whiskey bottle and the next morning, they found him dead. They think he was too drunk to tell that it wasn't whiskey in the bottle. The family moved into town for the dog mushing season not long after that incident. It was hard starting a new school halfway through the school year. A few nights, the man didn't come home because he was out drinking. When he came home, he would try to cuddle with the boy and his sister and stink like whiskey. The boy had a weak stomach and felt like throwing up when the man breathed on him.

The following spring, they went back to the river to fish. The man still teased the boy. It seemed as if the teasing never stopped. The teasing was about everything from girls to calling him names. The boy looked forward to times when people would stop by to visit. He had to be careful about what he said, though, because the man liked to stretch the truth when he talked to people. If the boy innocently said something that was the truth that conflicted with what the man said, he was told to shut up. "Shut up" soon became one of the things that the man regularly told the boy to do. The boy started to lose confidence around other people, and he wasn't sure if he spoke that he would be humiliated or put down by the man.

That is the summer when the boy started to notice the alcohol. Living in a fish camp was a lot of work, and the boy learned to work hard. They would occasionally make trips to town for supplies. They would get groceries, and the man always had to have his beer supply. The boy once counted over twenty cases of beer stacked behind the cabin. The man started wanting the boy and girl to call him dad. The boy wouldn't, as the man wasn't his dad. The man teased him, and the boy couldn't stand the smell of the man when he tried to hug him while he was drunk.

That winter, they stayed in a plywood shack that didn't have insulation. The fire had to be kept going all the time, full blast, or the wind would make it so cold you could see your breath. At night, they would have to bundle up in several sleeping bags to stay warm through the night. The man would make the boy get up in the cold and build a fire, while the man would have whiskey in his coffee in the morning after the cabin started to warm. The boy and the girl took correspondence courses for school. The man went into town once to check the mail and didn't come back for several days because he got drunk. A teacher came part way through the winter and tested the boy and the girl on their schoolwork and then left several books for them to read. As the boy learned to read better, he lost himself in the books to escape the man's meanness.

Leaving camp in mid-winter for the dog mushing race season was exciting. One of the highlights for the boy was going to the races and getting to compete in the junior races. The *family had started to build a log home in town that year so they would have a place to stay when they came to town. Now, the man even teased the boy about his schoolwork; he would call him "Little Einstein," along with the other teasing. The boy also loved to play games with his mom and sister because it was a way to get away from the reality of the man and his drinking.*

Research supports the transformation people experience when writing. Numerous studies have been conducted on the benefits of journaling. JAMA published a study conducted in the late 1990s that found that when asthma and rheumatoid arthritis patients were asked to journal 20 minutes a day, they showed improvement in their symptoms. Interestingly, some patients were asked to journal about stressful events, and others were asked to journal their plans for the day. Although both groups showed improvement, it was highest for those journaling about the stressful events.[5] The Reflection App cites several studies and reasons why journaling is important, including helping with depression and anxiety symptoms, increasing immune function, and developing gratitude. It also helps one recover from trauma and memory function. Recent studies have focused on using journaling to help children improve mental health symptoms, promote positive feelings, and improve academic skills.

To get better at anything – sports, school, and work – we must be willing to admit where we are starting, to be honest with ourselves. You love members of your family, and it can be hard to say that your dad used drugs or your grandma had an alcohol use disorder. You may not even have recognized it, especially as a child. This understanding can have so many layers to it, including stigma and shame. Remember that you are not betraying them;

you are simply stating facts. Saying the words tied to trauma are not easy words to say. Words hold power as they possess the ability to influence and impact others by shaping thoughts, emotions, and actions. While we do not want to sit in a victim mentality, we need to be honest with ourselves. We are generally drawn to authentic people, so why would we not be real with ourselves? For some people, being honest with themselves is the hardest step. In his book, *The Body Keeps the Score*, Dr. Van der Kolk described how his former teacher, Elvin Semrad, would explain how "most human suffering is related to love and loss" and how "The greatest sources of our suffering are the lies we tell ourselves."[6] A clue to better understanding ourselves may be topics or situations you avoid or memories triggered by the sound of sirens.

I organized this book with each chapter being a stand-alone story examining a challenging time and a lesson that came with it. I follow the story with a thought you can carry with you, and I end the chapter with journal prompts and space for you to examine your thoughts, feelings, and actions. When you journal, please don't worry about complete sentences and grammar. When you journal, get the thoughts out of your head so you can begin to recognize thoughts that you may want to explore deeper.

Thought to Carry with You

"Take care of the old person you are going to become."
– Walter Soboleff, Tlingit Elder and Scholar

JOURNAL PROMPTS

1. If you don't journal, what is keeping you from journaling? What would make it possible for you to journal regularly? Are you open to keeping a journal or at least writing down some thoughts after each chapter?

_____

_____

_____

_____

_____

_____

_____

_____

_____

_____

_____

_____

_____

_____

_____

_____

_____

_____

2. What is a favorite childhood memory?

3. Is there something in your life you would like to change and why?

_____

_____

_____

_____

_____

_____

_____

_____

_____

_____

_____

_____

_____

_____

_____

_____

_____

_____

_____

_____

_____

Chapter 2

THE ACCIDENT

While you are watching your favorite hour-long show, someone will die due to a person's decision to drink and drive. According to the National Highway Traffic Safety Administration on crashes, in 2022, 13,524 people died in the United States (US) due to alcohol-impaired driving. In the US, 32% of all traffic fatalities are due to alcohol-impaired driving. To put that in perspective, one person will die every 39 minutes.[1] Unfortunately, I learned about the consequences as a teenager.

In 1981, I was a typical junior high school student, full of doubts about myself. I was excited that one of the popular girls had invited me to a Halloween party that weekend. I arrived home from school that Friday afternoon to hurry and complete my chores, as I would be attending a football game that night. I had joined the band, and we were scheduled to perform at halftime.

My family had a dairy farm, so no one was exempt from chores, and the fall meant harvest time. The high level of rainfall had made the fall harvest challenging. My mom had agreed to watch my cousin's baby girl at our house, and my dad was trying to handle the milking duties while my brother and his friend continued work on the harvest.

As I was preparing to leave with my mom to take me to school, my dad said he needed her to come to the barn to take over milking the cows. My brother had run into equipment problems in the field and needed Dad's help. It was getting dark, so we would be racing against time. My grandmother, who lived with us, had been talking with the baby and offered to give me a ride while my younger sister babysat. Dad left for the fields, Mom headed to the barn, and Grandma and I walked to the car.

I got into the car with an uneasy feeling. My dad had been so urgent about the equipment situation that I thought maybe something else was wrong. I hoped no one was hurt, but I couldn't shake the emotions I felt. Grandma and I were mostly quiet on the ride. I thought I would be late, but hopefully only by a few minutes.

I closed my eyes to ask God to keep my brother and father safe. I opened my eyes. Suddenly, I saw a flash of light and then nothing. I felt a heaviness, like I was in a fog and something was sitting on me. Loud saw sounds that reminded me of my dad's chainsaws, the banging of metal coming together, and flashing lights overtook my senses. I could hear someone saying, "Easy, easy, don't move her back!" I was trying to open my eyes but couldn't quite keep them open. I felt cold, really cold.

A man in a uniform must have seen my eyes flutter as he quietly told me, "It's okay; it will be okay. You were in an accident." He asked if I knew my name.

"Yes," I responded, "I can't feel anything. I am really cold." They covered me with more blankets just before I felt them lift me into the ambulance.

I asked the paramedic, "Where is my grandma?"

"They are taking care of her." He responded.

Darkness overtook me again until I felt them lowering me down. The whirl of people and activity was almost too much – cutting clothes, moving me for exams and x-rays, and asking questions. I still felt cold. I asked a nurse for more blankets. During a pause in the activity, a man who appeared to be a chaplain entered the room. I noticed he seemed a bit distant, but I felt like the fog in my brain was lifting enough that I wanted to know what had happened.

"Sir, would you please tell me what happened? How did I end up here?" I asked.

"There was an accident, but it appears the gentleman in the other car is far worse off," he responded with a disgusted look.

What did the chaplain mean? Before I could inquire, he abruptly left the room. Why did he seem to think the accident might be my fault? I was confused. All I knew was I couldn't get warm, and my entire body hurt.

Not long after the chaplain left, Mom and Dad entered the room. I was having a hard time reading their faces. Mom looked like she was trying to control her emotions. Dad looked like he was having an internal battle with himself. A doctor came in, and he talked mainly with Mom and Dad. The doctor also seemed confused but relieved. He explained how it appeared my injuries were far worse when I came in. But as of that moment, they were not finding any broken bones, only contusions, swelling, and cuts. He told my parents he felt I should spend the night in the hospital because I should be monitored after being unconscious for so long. The doctor left, and Dad stepped outside as well. Only Mom and I remained in the room.

"Mom, where's Grandma?" I asked.

Mom paused, then said, "She passed away."

"*What*?" I thought I didn't hear her correctly. "You mean she died?" I asked, hoping I was wrong.

"Yes," She quietly responded.

I felt disbelief and shock. My face was full of glass, and cuts hurt as the tears streamed down my face. I was trying not to sob because I could see my mom was trying to hold herself together. A few hospital staff took me to a room, and Mom told me they would be back in the morning. She left.

I had never felt so alone. I felt confused, scared, and so very tired. Sleep overtook me. When I woke up in the wee hours of the morning, my brain was less foggy, but I was still unsure of what had happened. I felt dirty and sticky. I waited for the nurse and asked if I could take a shower. She indicated that it might not be possible because of all my stitches, but she would get back to me.

A person passed by with a cart and asked if I wanted a newspaper. "Yes," I said. But then he asked for payment. I realized I had no money, no anything – none of my clothes or possessions, and I had no idea when my parents were coming. Once again, I felt alone and scared.

The nurse returned and told me I couldn't shower yet, but she could help me wash up. For the first time since the accident, I saw myself in the mirror. My face was full of cuts. My hair was matted in clumps. As the nurse helped me stand at the sink, I saw blood mixing with the dirt and water. My legs almost gave out under my weight as I realized that the blood might not be just my blood but my grandma's.

As I returned to my bed, I realized that I somehow had a copy of the newspaper. I thought the person sharing the room heard me ask but sensed I would not be able to purchase it. I saw the article; it was not long, but it told of my grandmother's death. The man who crossed the centerline to hit us was a neighbor. He had just left the bar before the accident occurred.

Losing my grandmother changed my life forever. I told no one of my internal battles and tried to pretend everything was okay, but everything had changed. Sirens started to scare me. When I heard sirens, I stopped what I was doing. It was so intuitive that there was no thought, just response. I took a deep breath and said a silent prayer, "God, please take this pain and fear away."

A flurry of activity took place in preparation for my grandma's funeral. Family came, friends stopped by and brought meals, all while I pretended to be okay. I learned that the chaplain at the hospital had assumed I was the teenage driver who hit the other car since my grandmother's body had been taken to a different hospital. I also learned that they initially thought I had broken my back, arm, and leg, which is why the doctor seemed confused. My friends told me that our pastor and several members of our church's teen choir had met together to pray for me after learning I was injured in the accident.

Knowing my parents were overwhelmed and did not like the extra attention, I tried to be okay. I even chased and played with my younger cousin at the family gathering after my grand-ma's funeral. I ran by my dad and our pastor, but I froze inside when I overheard my dad say, "It could have been Carol." For the first time, it struck me that my grandma took my mom's place that night. My nightmares began to fluctuate from replaying my grandma's death to my mom dying instead. I struggled with the guilt that I was the one who needed the ride. The quiet pain con-tinued.

A few months later, in December, my older sister and I at-tended a weekend camp retreat for our church's teen choir. I was still trying to be okay. During an evening Bible study, our pastor shared the passage in Matthew on forgiveness and how God has called us to forgive others, even when we don't feel like it. I stayed after and told the pastor, "I don't feel like forgiving, but you just told us God instructs us to forgive."

He gently told me, "Cathy, I know it doesn't make sense, but even if you thought of the worst thing in the world to do against this person, it wouldn't make you feel better. Evil would win twice: once, from the action that happened against you, and twice because of the bitter feelings that take over your thoughts and life, robbing you of the joy in your life. Let's pray that God helps you release it and forgive. I have seen how often the people that com-mit the bad manage to wreck their lives worse than we could ever think of doing."

Peace came over me as we prayed. I would never have to agree that what the man who hit us did was okay, but I could forgive him.

The current drunk driving laws did not exist at the time. Our neighbor only received six months in jail for killing my grandma.

His injuries had taken months to heal. I felt awful for my younger sister, who had been close friends with the man's youngest son. The accident created an awkwardness in their relationship that had not been there before the accident.

Around a year later, I was at home with my siblings after school when we heard sirens again. This time, the sirens headed to the neighbor's house. The man, who was home from prison, had struggled with his eldest son in an attempt to commit suicide. Although both survived, it created even more trauma for their family. As my older sister and I talked, I felt true sadness for the man and his family. I shared what the pastor had shared with me and realized how the man had managed to wreck his life.

A few years later, I was home from college and driving my younger sister home from church. Not far from the church, a man was hitchhiking. I decided to help him out and give him a ride. I asked him where he needed to go, and a little chit-chat ensued. I noticed he got quiet when he realized who our parents were. He quietly said, "They are good people."

I dropped him off at the requested corner. As we continued the drive, my sister turned to me, incredulous, and asked, "You do realize who that was, right?"

It had been the very same man who killed my grandma a few years before. I knew at that point I would always miss my grandma, but I had learned what real forgiveness felt like in action. I know I will eventually hear sirens again, but I understand what it is like to be at peace with my past.

Forgiveness is a tricky subject. People don't think much about it until they are in the middle of it, whether they are the one needing forgiveness or the one needing to ask for it. People can struggle with forgiveness, often confusing the idea that forgiveness means you are okay with what happened versus separating the actions from the person. However, the release and the relief forgiveness ultimately gives us is what makes it worth doing. Yu'pik Grandmother Rita Pitka Blumenstein of the International Council of Thirteen Grandmothers shared, "God said there is only abundance, and the only way through is to forgive. Holding on to negative emotions becomes cancer or another illness. Our healing is not just for ourselves, it is for the universe."[2]

I would be lying if I told you that sharing the story doesn't make me relive it. Yet, almost every month, I share my story on a victim's impact panel where people who have been convicted of driving under the influence (DUI) attend. I hope that someone hearing my story will remember it at the right time, and it will help them make a better decision.

As my children entered their teenage years, I knew peer pressure would begin to factor into decisions to party. We had candid discussions about how they might find themselves in situations where it would be hard to say no to trying alcohol. I wanted to be sure they knew, above all things, never to drive drunk or get into a vehicle with someone who had been drinking. They could say their mom would ground them if she ever found out or any other story they wanted to make up to save face with their friends. I also assured them they could call me, and I would come right away with no questions. We would eventually need to discuss it, but it wouldn't have to be that night.

My children were tested and sometimes did not make the best decisions, but they knew never to drive drunk, as it had been drilled into their thinking. Sometimes, they did reach out for help with a late-night call. I learned I had to lead with love and grace in those situations, not fear and what-ifs.

Alcohol can become a habit, an addiction, a pain reliever, or a coping strategy that leads to dark consequences, whether hurting oneself or others. During my panel talks, I hear over and over how people are so thankful they didn't hurt anyone while they were driving drunk. Our facilitator skillfully helps them think through what it does cost, even if they haven't hurt or killed someone – yet. You can experience court costs, higher insurance rates, lost jobs, damaged relationships, and your inner voice that might torment you. Even without injuring anyone, NHTSA estimates that first-time offenders can spend upwards of $10,000 in fines and legal fees.[3] I hope hearing my story might help people make a different decision next time. Our mistakes do not have to define us if we choose to make a different decision when faced with the same situation.

Despite the passage of time, sirens still make me pause and pray. The sirens no longer scare me like they did at first after the accident. In the early years following the accident, sirens would trigger fear and panic, and I would have to rationalize myself through the anxious feelings. Now, I simply remind myself that everything will probably be okay and say a quick prayer. Occasionally, the siren will catch me on a day when I am in a melancholy mood, and I replay the events, thinking about the people in my story. I reflect on how hundreds have heard my story. I think of the young woman who shared how my story made her cry, not just from my pain but from the beauty of forgiveness. To forgive, we decide whether we are going to continue to allow the past to control our future or whether we release anger, hurt, and pain. Forgiveness allows us to focus on living, not what was taken away.

Thought to Carry with You

"The difference between who you are and who you want
to be is what you do."
– Bill Phillips, from his book *Body for Life: 12 Weeks to
Mental and Physical Strength*

JOURNAL PROMPTS

1. Have you ever driven drunk? Have you ever been a passenger
   in a vehicle with someone who had been drinking and was
   now driving? How might your decision be different now
   than it was then? Even if you haven't, what are some things
   you can do to ensure you don't find yourself in one of those
   situations? What can you do if you do find yourself in that
   situation?

---

2. Do you have any "sirens" from your past that bring up painful thoughts or memories? Have you talked to someone about the memories? Have you journaled about the painful thoughts? Remember, resources exist, and people are available to help you.

_____

_____

_____

_____

_____

_____

_____

_____

_____

_____

_____

_____

_____

_____

_____

_____

_____

_____

Resources

After reading this chapter, you may have realized that you need help, or perhaps you know someone who drinks too much. Here are some resources you can use to help.

Crisis? Please call or text 988 to talk to someone.

- A general informational resource is SAMHSA (Substance Abuse and Mental Health Services Administration.

  https://www.samhsa.gov/find-help/national-helpline

  1-800-662-4357

- Another general starting point is AA (Alcoholics Anonymous). You can find a local contact at aa.org.

- The National Institute on Aging has some helpful information on how, as our bodies change, the impact of alcohol can as well. The website also discusses how medications can influence how alcohol impacts the body.

  https://www.nia.nih.gov/health/how-help-someone-you-know-who-drinks-too-much

- Many of our veterans have seen and experienced trauma, and many choose to self-medicate with alcohol. Resources now exist to help.

  https://www.maketheconnection.net/conditions/alcohol-use-disorder

  Helping Yourself from Veterans Pages

  https://www.maketheconnection.net/resources/self-help

Chapter 3

THE WINDOW

Tucked high in a century-year-old barn is a window where I spent hours as a youth examining the world and day-dreaming about what life could be like in my future. The same window showed the dark, ominous clouds that would carry our neighbor's world away in a tornado. The tornado taught me how, collectively, a community's world can change overnight, yet the rest of the world could keep moving like nothing had changed.

As a youth, I would walk through the metal door over the chaff-covered floor and past the feed bins to find the tall wooden ladder leading to the hay loft, approximately 12 feet above the floor. Ascending the ladder, I would notice the large beam, which had the only light source mounted to it, and see that the straw mow was to my right, and the first and second cut hay was to the left. At the top, I would step off the ladder onto a dense, thick beam that supported the main structure of the barn. Climbing into the first cutting hay mow in the fall and early winter, I would be close to the highest peak in the barn. The roof was slanted, made of single wooden planks, and covered with large slate shingles. Cobwebs hung in varying shapes and sizes from the antique pulleys and haylifts. When I reached the right wall of the mow, there was a window that let me examine the world perched high above everything else on the farm. I spent countless hours thinking about the world and daydreaming by the window.

After having a rough or frustrating day, I would cry or think out my feelings in solitude by the window. I would react to many of my life's situations, usually finding solutions. God and I had some of my best talks while I sat on the hay bale and observed His wonderwork. I could see the acres of fields and pastures lined with woods, all snow-covered and lying peacefully in contrast with the shadows from the trees. Like nature-inspired Christmas lights, light beams streamed down from the moon while the stars danced in the sky above the snow.

As the snow melted, so did the haymow; soon, I would not be able to see out the window until next winter when the hay had been restacked from the hours of work over the summer. Little did I know that the very place where I found peace would be the same place I would hear the power of destruction.

On Friday, May 31, 1985, I was a junior in high school at Northwestern Senior High in Albion, Pennsylvania. Spring was moving into summer, and we were all looking forward to the end of the school year. The school was buzzing as our high school softball team was on fire and had recently won enough games that they were moving on to districts. I had several friends on the team and was excited about their game on Saturday. I remember leaving high school with one of my friends. We were talking about how hot and humid it was. My friend commented on how still the air felt. I remember pausing and saying, "You know you're right.

There's not a breeze to be found. Feels weird, doesn't it?" Later, I would learn that the stillness and heaviness we felt were signs of what was coming.

I was ready for the school year to be done, but we still had a few more days with end-of-school activities planned and graduation scheduled for Thursday. As I drove home, I thought about my upcoming vacation and summer job. I was a farm kid, and I had been taught that chores had to be done before anything else. I knew that the dairy cows on our farm didn't care what else was happening in our lives; they had to be taken care of and milked every day. The late afternoon continued to be hot, and I dreaded putting on the heavy jeans to climb into the hay mow, where I knew it would be even hotter. I must have been moving a little too slow for my dad, as he sent one of the hired hands to help me. The sky darkened while pitching hay out of the mow, and we knew a storm was brewing. At one point, the hired hand, a long-time family friend, stopped pitching hay and said, "That plane sounds more like a train. They must be flying low because of the weather." I acknowledged that it seemed strangely loud. It wouldn't be long before we would discover that the noise had not been a plane.

Not long after our descent from the mow and moving on to other chores, our neighbor drove uncharacteristically fast into our yard, frantically talking to my dad and brother while his son, the hired hand, jumped into the truck as they took off down the road. Both my dad and brother looked upset, and I came to ask what was wrong. My brother said a tornado had touched down and destroyed our friend's farm and homes. It was a mess, and folks were missing. My older sister and I told our dad and brother to go help with the people and animals. They might need equipment and help. We would try to finish milking as quickly as possible, hoping the electricity would not go out. We knew the loss of life was likely, and it left a heaviness in the air.

We had a radio on in the barn, and tornado warnings blared out, but we all knew they had come too late for our neighbors. We sent our little sister to the house to put the television on – we were desperate for news. We focused on getting the chores done as quickly and efficiently as possible while the situation's weight stayed heavy in the air. Our mother had been working in a nearby community as a nurse and left work to shop for groceries. We were worried she might have unexpectedly run into the storm as the news indicated storm cells were appearing in several places. Our sister came to the barn crying. She said, "The tornado has hit Albion, and it's bad, really bad." Albion was a small community. If you didn't know someone there, you knew someone who did. We were all thinking of friends and family and wondering if they had made it.

We finished chores and gathered in the kitchen, watching the news coverage with tears streaming down our eyes in disbelief. I distinctly remember my mom pulling into the driveway. We flooded her with questions and information. I remember telling her that we needed to go. My mom, always the practical nurse, responded, "Cathy, they have first responders. We don't want to get in the way." It was the only time I can remember in my child-hood truly back talking to my mother. I told her she was a nurse. There was no way there were enough medical personnel with the destruction in Albion. Didn't she want to help people if she could? I thought that was what being a nurse was. I demanded we go to the neighbors, and if she wouldn't drive, I would. My sisters stood inside the house, shocked at my courage to speak to my mother that way. It was not the norm and generally not acceptable. To my surprise, my mom told me to get in the car, and we left. We drove in silence.

Only a few miles down the road, it changed; everything looked the same as it always had until it didn't. Trees had been ripped apart, leaving tall stumps mixed with debris from the homes and barns the storm had destroyed. The sound of saws and equipment running and voices yelling as they attempted to round up disoriented farm animals all blended with this new reality. With one look at my mom, I knew she had not expected the degree of destruction we encountered. The devastation was so vast you didn't know where to look first. A neighbor gave us a quick update: one of our neighbors had been in the car with her elderly mother trying to leave as they knew her house trailer would never survive. The neighbor survived, but the tornado had ripped her elderly mother right from the car, tossing her and ultimately killing her. Another family had made it to their basement but had suffered injuries from being struck by parts of their collapsing home. The injured were being driven in personal vehicles as every available emergency response unit had headed to the more populated area of Albion.

Not long before our arrival, they had found the body of one of my brother's best friend's wife. She had put the dog in the car, and they assumed she was attempting to outrun the storm. Unfortunately, her car was found on the other side of the neighbor's silo. It had taken a while for her husband to arrive from work. The debris and location of her car meant he needed to drive a tractor across several fields to reach her. His cries were mournful and went right to our hearts. I remember fighting back the tears as I did not want my mom to think I was not strong enough to handle the scene. Someone must have asked my mom for help, and I continued forward, eventually finding my brother to ask if I could help with anything. He said that now that the people were accounted for, it was mainly relocating the animals, and several local farmers, including my dad, were helping with it. My brother started to share stories of the chaos they encountered and filled me in on what they had pieced together had happened. As we walked toward one of the piles of debris that had been a part of the barn, I stopped and asked, "What is that smell? I have never smelled anything like this." My brother turned, looked me in the eye with tears in the corner of his, and said, "Cathy, that is the smell of death." I stood speechless and simply nodded my head. I understood I was experiencing something that would stay with me for the rest of my life.

Darkness was moving in, and it was agreed that all the neighbors had been accounted for. Other neighbors and family were taking the folks that needed places to stay. Plans were made for regrouping in the morning, but because insurance companies would need to be involved, they would mainly focus on clearing the road. Word had reached the group that Albion had been decimated. One of the neighbors said it reminded him of a war zone. It was not hard to believe after looking at the destruction before us.

My dad and brother were exhausted as we sat trying to eat supper with all the emotions running through us. We were glued to the television and a little on edge as we awaited word from friends and family. Rumors were running wild on the estimated number of deaths because the tornado had touched down on Main Street at 5:15 PM, just as most folks were sitting down to dinner. The funnel cloud had started near us in a reign of terror 14 miles long and 400 yards wide. NOAA estimated the tornado to be an F4 devastating tornado with winds between 207-260 mph.[1] Our town had many older Victorian-style homes built in the late 1800s and early 1900s. Many homes and businesses were gone, taken by the winds.

We also learned that several other tornadoes had hit the region, destroying smaller communities. Tornadoes had touched down in Ohio, Pennsylvania, New York, and Ontario, Canada. My mom reminded us not to believe everything the news was posting. We wanted to help, but they asked people to stay away so the emergency crew could do their job. Gas valves needed to be shut off, and electrical wires needed to be sorted out to help keep the destruction from worsening.

Dad and my brother shared stories of what the evening had entailed for them. My dad spoke with admiration in his voice as he shared how one of our neighbors had ridden his horse to help round up the animals and search places that might be hard for equipment to enter. The neighbor had come across a cow that was on fire and was burning itself to death as it ran. His skill and marksmanship came into play as he galloped on the horse and used his pistol to put the animal out of its misery. Stories of adrenaline-fueled heroic efforts abounded.

My high school had turned into a morgue; the junior high school had become the Red Cross shelter, where folks could find a warm meal, basic supplies, and a place to sleep if needed. The National Guard had been called in and was also being housed at the junior high. The television news and the newspaper brought much-needed information outside the barb-wire the National Guard had placed around the community to keep people from entering. We learned that the trailer parks had all been destroyed, but the one in the sister community, Cranesville, had been destroyed, claiming three lives, including a pregnant mom. Several older people had been killed, all in different situations, but all caught unexpectedly. One of the more heart-wrenching stories from Albion was the six-year-old boy who died in his pregnant mom's arms as a collapsing wall crushed them. She could feel him taking his last breaths and told him, "Go to sleep." Miraculously, his mom and siblings survived. In all, twelve people had been killed in our local area. The total number of deaths from all the tornadoes in the region grew to 89 people in total, injuring over 1,000 and causing over $600 million in damage.[1]

Some of our high school softball team members had lost their homes, and several more had been impacted. The softball coach reached out to the players who had lost their homes and explained they did not have to play in the district championships on Saturday, but everyone wanted to play. Finding gear and uniforms was challenging, but thankfully, two sisters who had lost their home had put their uniforms in the laundry and located the dryer amid the wreckage to retrieve their uniforms. The team arrived two hours late for the game as it had taken some time to get everyone together for the bus ride to the game. Less than twenty-four hours after the tornado ripped through the town, the courageous young women dug past the exhaustion and emotions to play together, facing the number one team in the county. They were down 6-4 after the fourth inning, but they dug deep and won 18-7! The victory reminded everyone what can be accomplished when we work together. They were truly representing their community, which was back home doing just that amid the destruction. The opposing coach felt no one could have beaten our girls that day.

Our local Albion, Pennsylvania newspaper at the time, *The Albion News*, created a special edition to help document the historic event and pulled together information on services, cancellations, meetings, resources, and thank you's. The special edition also included a map of destroyed homes and businesses as well as a list of the injured and their current status at the hospital. They also included the obituaries of those who died in the tornado. The editor attempted to address some of the emotions in his editorial, acknowledging the struggles of asking why this tragedy occurred.

Following the shock were waves of emotions that included anger and frustration. A volunteer fireman was credited for saving lives due to his emergency radio warning after spotting the funnel. Many families in the area had scanners to hear the warning; unfortunately, many did not. The fire department sirens blared, but only briefly, as the power was cut off. Warning systems were available but not in place. It felt like the rest of the world kept going about their normal business, but our community members needed to figure out the new normal, and it was challenging.

The help politicians promised in the aftermath felt like a huge bureaucracy. This was a puzzle the community members had a difficult time solving. People were frustrated with the mixed messages on state and federal aid; many did not have the necessary documents to complete forms. The focus stayed on rebuilding the community, but many people also needed help recovering from the emotional side. Many people suffered from survivor's guilt.

According to a 2023 study published in *Cureus*, survivor's guilt is "the response to an event that some people experience when they survive a traumatic event or situation that others did not."[2] Survivor's guilt can be associated with post-traumatic stress disorder (PTSD), anxiety, and complicated grief. Frequently, a survivor's guilt gets overlooked because of other related symptoms. It is essential to understand that it can be its own psychological phenomenon, often but not always with PTSD.

More resources and awareness are now available for addressing the mental health aspects of a disaster compared to the past. The small town leaned heavily on the churches in the area, and some counseling services were made available, but most tried to walk it through the best they could with the tools they had. People react to natural disaster losses differently. For some people, their resilience grows; for others, the trauma sends them into an unstoppable mental spiral.

Natural disasters will cause emotional distress, and for many people it will be temporary, only lasting a few days. Others, especially children and teens, may suffer for an extended period of time. Often, the children and youth struggle with wanting things to be "normal" again. You find that symptoms do not show up immediately but appear a few weeks or months after the event. Some warning signs that you or someone you love may be experiencing emotional distress after a natural disaster are trouble sleeping and concentrating or finding yourself angry, sad, frustrated, and feeling hopeless.[3] Do not wait to seek help. Resources are available. SAMHSA offers resources for parents and teachers to talk to children and youth after a natural disaster. You can reach the Disaster Distress Helpline at 1-800-985-5990 or www.disasterdistress.samhsa.gov.

At the time of the tornadoes, our small communities of Albion and Cranesville had a large number of volunteer first responders – both firefighters and emergency medical technicians. Many volunteers lost their homes and were impacted by the injuries and deaths that occurred. Looking back, there was a good chance that many of the local first responders dealt with what is now known as Compassion Fatigue. Compassion Fatigue happens when first responders are physically and emotionally tested and develop burnout and secondary traumatic stress. SAMHSA defines Compassion Fatigue like this: "When experiencing burnout, you may feel exhausted and overwhelmed, like nothing you do will help make the situation better. For some responders, the negative effects of this work can make them feel like the trauma of the people they are helping is happening to them or the people they love. This is called secondary traumatic stress." [4] If Compassion Fatigue is left unchecked, it can, over time, create more challenging mental health illness.[5]

It is important to remember that we don't have to "tough it out" when we experience trauma like a natural disaster. After the tornado in Albion, nature was silent for days afterward, but eventually, the songbirds returned and began to sing again. We may need to seek help when the world feels off, but with counseling or professional help, we will begin to feel more like ourselves again.

In the days following the tornado, I was in the hay mow again. Although the window in the barn remained and much of what I viewed from the window looked the same, I realized that the events of the past few days would make it so that I would never look at the world the same again. I was forever changed.

Thought to Carry with You

"Courage is always rewarded." – Kenny Loggins

Musician Kenny Loggins played a concert in Erie, Pennsylvania (the closest big city to Albion), the weekend after the tornados had struck the region. He donated concert proceeds to assist the tornado victims.

JOURNAL PROMPTS

1. Do you have any events from your past where your world
    seemed to stop while the rest of the world kept moving? If
    so, have you considered you may have some unprocessed
    thoughts about the event? If not, has anyone in your family
    experienced a significant event like a natural disaster? Have
    you thought about how it may have impacted them? If the
    event is emotionally charged, our bodies can create a stress
    response right after the event or much later. Rest and a
    healthy diet can help our bodies process the event. Please
    take a few minutes and journal, reminding yourself there is
    no right or wrong way to do it.

_____

_____

_____

_____

_____

_____

_____

_____

_____

_____

_____

_____

_____

_____

2. Have you ever suffered from survivor's guilt? It is often part of a PTSD diagnosis, but it does not have to be. Journaling about the situation can help identify some parts of your experience you may still need help unpacking. Have you considered learning some breathing techniques to help you as you deal with anxiety that can occur as you walk through processing your past? Don't be afraid to contact a friend or professional to talk about what you are processing.

_____

_____

_____

_____

_____

_____

_____

_____

_____

_____

_____

_____

_____

_____

_____

_____

_____

_____

Resources

If you need help with dealing with past trauma, please know there is help.

Crisis? Please call or text 988 to talk to someone.

- If you or someone you love experiences trouble sleeping and concentrating or you find yourself angry, sad, frustrated, and hopeless after experiencing a disaster, reach out to the Disaster Distress Helpline at 1-800-985-5990 or www.disasterdistress.samhsa.gov.

- A general informational resource is SAMHSA (Substance Abuse and Mental Health Services Administration. https://www.samhsa.gov/find-help/national-helpline or 1-800-662-4357

Chapter 4

THE OUTHOUSE

S ometimes, life doesn't go the way you plan. You need help, and it takes courage to ask for it. Only three years into my marriage, I went from living in a familiar place with a support system to what seemed like the middle of nowhere, lacking the knowledge I needed for a new lifestyle and only having an infant and toddler with whom to interact. I learned the hard way that stress and anxiety will cause alarms within our body that, when left unattended, will eventually get our attention.

In September of 1997, my husband and I started relocating our two-year-old daughter, two-month-old infant daughter, and sled dogs from Fairbanks, Alaska, to a more remote location in the interior, Eureka, Alaska. In early October, a friend helped me bring the last of what we could pack into her truck, and we headed north. The last few months had been a whirlwind – giving birth to our second daughter, deciding to sell our home, trying to find a place to relocate for my husband to train his team of sled dogs, mounting debts, and selling vehicles to afford a down payment on a four-wheel drive truck. I was doing all those things while trying to breastfeed a new infant, care for a toddler, pack, and clean the house. I did pretty well at saying my goodbyes, as I expected to see everyone when we came to town, but when I said goodbye to the babysitter, I cried. She and her husband had been so kind and loved our children. I was going to miss their support.

Remote living didn't just mean living several hours away from Fairbanks; it meant no electricity or running water, an outhouse, and a wood stove to keep going. Having been raised on a dairy farm, I knew how to work hard, but we had always had electricity. We needed the electricity to milk the cows and keep the milk cooled and clean until it could be transported to market. I was not an experienced outdoors wilderness person. I had never been camping with my family because of the farm. I could drive tractors, plant and harvest fields, care for animals every day – morning and night – but sleeping in a tent in the wilderness was not a part of my experiences. Thankfully, I had worked at a summer camp and gained some outdoor skills. I enjoyed hiking with friends and had lived in a log cabin before. But I was still inadequately prepared for what I was facing. My husband already had more than enough to do, and teaching was not one of his gifts, so we got off to a rough start because I simply did not have the knowledge I needed to survive out there. I learned to figure things out quickly, but some lessons were rough. I was grateful for the large cabin that had two bedrooms and a living area. An excerpt from my journal five days after moving reflects what I was experiencing:

> *Things are going okay. I still struggle not to complain and deal with the no water situation. I am doing well except for the outhouse – it's just so cold. I'm keeping so much inside, having no one to talk to – it makes my stomach hurt. I don't*

dare say anything to my husband as he would view it as complaining, and his grandmother, who lives in the village about 20 miles away, has dealt with so much worse that I won't even think of saying anything to her. I know I can handle it, but it doesn't mean I must like it. I am learning there is a fine line because I don't want to become resentful. The upside of things is that it is so peaceful here and beautiful. The snow-capped mountains talk to a person in all their grandeur. The northern lights are so incredible as there are no lights to hide them. I really like being with the dogs. When you don't have many people around to talk to – you talk to the dogs a lot more.

People fantasize about living out in the woods, not realizing how many daily chores need to be done just to survive. I was so excited when my husband got a generator working, which meant we had lights, a radio, and even an occasional VCR video for a few hours a day. We could only get one AM radio station that brought information from the outside world. It could be a bit staticky sometimes, but listening to it helped distract me from some of the more mundane tasks.

In November, I was outside using the outhouse and shutting off the generator for the night when I walked out to the most incredible display of northern lights I had ever seen. I felt as if I jumped high, I might be able to touch them. The ribbon of colors swirled around, and I thought for a minute that they might swoop down and capture us in their dance. I remember hearing this sound, like a crackling, but I couldn't quite figure it out. I called for my husband, and he came to the cabin door.

I asked, "Do you hear that?"

"Yes, Cathy," he replied. "That is the northern lights talking."

He promptly shut the door like this was no big deal. I stood in awe in the midst of them for a few more minutes, praying and thanking God for creating this unique creation and allowing me to be a part of it. I felt like I was being rewarded for working so hard every day.

Fortunately, the folks whose cabin we were staying in came out several times from Fairbanks to their place, only a short drive away. They also had a two-year-old daughter and would often take our daughter to play. Our daughter would miss them when they would head to town and not return for several weeks. Potty training is a lot different when it involves an outhouse. I knew I wouldn't find much advice on that in parenting magazines. However, I was incredibly thankful when a friend told me I could sign up with the public library in Fairbanks so they could mail books to us. Even at 2 ½, our daughter would get excited to see the red mail pouch she knew would have new books for us to read.

The cold, dark, and isolation could be rough, but we had so many things to do we often did not get to bed until the wee hours of the morning. We would need to be back up fairly early to keep the fires going and get chores done. I was excited to learn that the village about twenty miles away via a dirt road had recently opened a washeteria where I could pay to do my laundry once a week and shower. I had to be careful with our money, but I could at least do the heavy clothes and only have to hand wash the lighter things that dried quickly in our cabin. The scrubboard worked better on some clothes than others. I treasured the $1.00 shower once a week. We were able to get drinking water there as well. I usually picked one day a week, and we would drive to the village to check our mail, do laundry, shower, and stop in to see my husband's grandparents.

Our nearest full-time neighbors, who lived a few miles up the road that turned into a trail in the winter, were wonderful. The wife would stop by once a week on her way into the village to check mail. She would almost always stop by to visit. Oh, how I treasured having another woman to talk to, especially one who knew how to do things around camp. She was able to help me with my propane tank and other tasks around the cabin. She was so kind and mainly just listened to me. I am not sure she knew she was my weekly therapist, but as a young wife and mother, I was struggling. She even took some of our pups to train, reducing my workload. Her visits were often the highlight of my week. She was a wonderful storyteller, too. I learned so much from her. I referred to her as one of my earth angels. The other earth angel was a single mom whose daughters were grown and out on their own. She lived outside the village and had a small team of sled dogs. She would occasionally pack her dog sled and drive her dog team out to us. She would stay for a few days to give me a break with the girls and help me catch up with chores.

By late December, I was doing okay with most tasks when my husband was gone, either training or racing. However, I was getting a little unnerved by the wolves in the area. I would mention something to my husband about feeling "watched" sometimes. He had seen their tracks but told me I would be fine. On Christmas Eve, we had our nearest neighbors over for dinner, and they started telling stories about wolves coming into their yards and killing their dogs a few years back. Everyone was noticing the number of wolves around the area.

One night, while my husband was away, I was getting ready for bed and had gone to shut the generator off in the shop and use the outhouse. I usually took our pet dog, a blue heeler, with me when I went. The kids were both sound asleep in the cabin. I must have been in routine mode, not thinking too much about what I was doing, but after a few moments of work, I noticed the blue heeler was acting funny. By the time we got to the outhouse, the blue heeler was glued to my leg and attempting to get in the outhouse with me. The heeler was not usually clingy, and I told her I didn't need her help, but she still kept trying to come into the outhouse with me. I did not think much about it until it dawned on me that the dog was afraid of something. I quickly did my business and opened the outhouse door. Once again, the heeler was glued to my leg. I turned briefly to look into the woods on the other side of the small creek behind the cabin and outhouse. Pairs of green-gold eyes stared back at me. I am not exactly sure how many wolves there were, but enough to know the dog and I were sorely outnumbered. I'm not sure who made it back to the cabin first – the dog or myself. I was breathing hard, and my heart was racing. Once safely in the cabin, the dog looked up as if to say, "See! I was trying to tell you. Next time, pay attention sooner!" You had better believe I learned not to ignore my pet dog when we were outside!

In January, my husband's sister was getting married. Not having anyone to help us with the dogs meant packing everyone up to head to town for a week. Daylight is scarce that time of year, and the cold makes daily tasks harder. We were trying to figure out all the logistics. My husband often worked things out in his head on his long training runs but would forget he still had to verbalize the details to me. I didn't automatically know what he wanted, and I was struggling because I was so tired. I just wanted to sleep. The baby still woke up every night and often acted like her tummy hurt. Our toddler slept hard once asleep but would battle me about going to sleep almost every night since the deep cold and wind kept us inside and made her restless.

I tried to juggle all the kennel chores while also managing doctor appointments, haircuts, and other family obligations related to the wedding. My husband was upset that I was trying to do different things besides the kennel to-dos. We were not communicating well. My sister-in-law was beautiful, and the wedding was wonderful, but I was falling apart. My husband and I had argued earlier that day. He still seemed angry at me and left the reception after eating, leaving me alone and hurt. I tried to have a good time, but deep down, I was miserable. I was beginning to wonder if something was wrong with me. I didn't want to go to the doctor because if they found something, I didn't want my husband to blame all our problems on me. I decided to read Grandma's herb book to see if I could find something that could help people suffering from the winter blues. An excerpt from my journal at the time reflects how I was thinking:

> I had a revelation today. I realize I have not been writing my thoughts down and recording my life because I would be facing reality. The reality that life wasn't always what I had made it out to be. It was easier to blame someone else for what happened in my life than to face the truth about how my decisions affected my life. Maybe it was the fear of recording my bad decisions or thoughts as I worked through things. I won't be around to explain or justify what others read after I die. I like journaling, but I don't think I have written every day since childhood. I know this is good ther-

apy and will help me clear my head and heart. Maybe being honest with myself would be a great place to start.

My tears were freezing as they fell from my eyes. I needed to return to the cabin where my seven-month-old and almost three-year-old lay sleeping. The deep snow and bitter wind only made the journey more painful. No one could hear my cries. My husband was away for work while I stayed with our children and sled dogs, hours away from medical care. My abdomen still ached as horrible cramps slowly subsided. My heart was squeezing in pain. I didn't need anyone to tell me: I had just lost our baby in our outhouse in the wilderness. I knew inside that emotionally I was hurting, but there wasn't anyone to tell. Once inside the cabin, I could see the blood; I lay on the bed and wept for the baby I would never hold, the loneliness and emptiness I felt. I told no one. I had rationalized that since I had only just suspected that I was pregnant and had not told anyone, I didn't need to tell anyone that I had lost a baby in an outhouse. I felt disgusted and sick. My journal entry from the time reflects my thinking:

> *I am flipping through pages of my journal and remembering how I had called out to God for help in the past and how alone I felt. Not long afterward, I read how I thought I had found the love of my life, and he had the characteristics I was looking for in a husband: hardworking, faithful, and honest. I would write about how I couldn't wait to see him again and felt safe and cherished in his arms. Now, I am reading harsh words, anger, and frustration. I am so sad. What is wrong with me? Why am I not seeing the good in things? I am so tired, God. Please help me.*

I started to realize how sad I was, and no matter how hard I tried, I could not get myself out of it. When I would bring it up, everyone would dismiss it as due to having a new baby, a toddler, sled dogs to care for, and living where life took a lot of work just to survive. I couldn't shake the thought that no matter how hard I try, I can't seem to feel better. So I did what I thought I was supposed to do and tried to get through my days and to-do list. Our marriage was struggling. My husband felt our marriage was a mistake, and I didn't know how to communicate my feelings. Honestly, if my husband had asked me what he could do to make me happy, I am not sure I would have had a response. I just knew I needed to hang on for my children.

As the light began to return with the spring, I finally had a chance to go to town to see a doctor. A dear friend had convinced me that perhaps the birth control I had been put on was affecting my feelings and weight. Sure enough, the new doctor confirmed that the birth control my old doctor had prescribed after having the baby had a high correlation with women experiencing postpartum depression. If I added the miscarriage in with that, my body had not found a hormonal balance yet. I couldn't see it on my own, but after the doctor explained postpartum depression and the varying degrees it can impact someone, I felt like someone had lifted a weight. I had an explanation. However, almost immediately, I felt a wave of shame when the doctor suggested I try a mild antidepressant. Did that mean I was weak and broken? Would I need it forever? The doctor reassured me that most people only needed it for three to six months to help their body recover. I remember leaving feeling relieved but like I was broken and needed fixing. Just like the experience of losing the baby, I didn't want to tell anyone.

Eventually, the medication started to help by removing some of the heaviness that had been weighing on me. My husband and

I had decided we needed to move closer to the main road system where medical care could be reached more quickly, and my husband could access the airport for a better commute to his job on the North Slope of Alaska. That decision opened up a whole new era, but at least I felt more of myself and did not spiral into sadness.

I now understand that medication can be used to help us. Our brains are complicated, so learning how to treat mental health disorders is often a trial and error on what works for an individual versus the collective. Most mental health medications do not heal us; they help us to find a level of control to be able to address the other challenges facing us. In his book, *The Body Keeps the Score*, Dr. Bessel Van Der Kolk discusses medications in healing from trauma: "However, drugs cannot 'cure' trauma; they can only dampen the expressions of a disturbed physiology. And they do not teach the lasting lessons of self-regulation. They can help to control feelings and behavior, but always at a price – because they work by blocking the chemical systems that regulate engagement, motivation, pain, and pleasure." He goes on to explain that what works for one patient may not be right for the next one.[1] I was fortunate that I only needed to take the medication for a few months before being able to get off it. I was physically active, and the warmer weather and sunshine helped my body. I could have done more internal work with someone, but at the time, I did not want anyone to know I was "broken" and needed help. We need to remember that mental health illnesses are as much of an illness as diseases such as diabetes or cancer. With the brain being so complex, it can take longer to find the right combination of medications. Just like we make lifestyle changes for other illnesses, it is good for us to explore healthy lifestyle changes that might help us with mental illnesses.

Depression is when you are feeling sad, withdrawn, or unmotivated for more than two weeks. It can be its own challenge, or it can be combined with other warning signs that it is time to ask for help. Are you experiencing any of the following?

- thinking of harming yourself
- suffering from severe mood swings
- reaching for drugs or alcohol to numb the pain
- engaging in out-of-control, risky behaviors
- experiencing drastic changes to your behavior
- dealing with sudden, unexplained, and overwhelming fear
- experiencing significant weight gain or loss
- unable to concentrate
- worrying enough that it impacts your daily activities

If you are experiencing these, it is time to reach out for help. You can often start with your regular doctor, who can refer you to someone else if they are not able to help. I will mention here that it is important to advocate for yourself or get someone to help you obtain the right help. My gut told me something wasn't right, and by switching doctors, I was able to get the help I needed.

Reflecting on that time period of my life, one of the greatest changes for me was my loss of daily connection with adults. I would sometimes have brief visits with people heading to the village of Rampart who would stop to park their vehicles or visit before they snowmachined to the village. (You could not drive to the village at the time.) We did have some friends come visit for a few days, and my sister-in-law and her family also came for a brief visit. At the time, I didn't realize how important it was to have interactions with other adults for my mental health. Connection is important and always has been.

Dr. Laverne Xilegg Demientieff is a clinical associate professor in social work who developed a framework called the Five C's of Healing Centered Engagement. She explains how the Five C's is a relational approach created in conjunction with learning from Indigenous Elders across Alaska on "how to apply cultural and traditional knowledge practices in our fast-paced modern society to benefit our collective health and wellness."[2] Her framework includes compassion, connection, community, curiosity, and ceremony. Dr. Demientieff focuses on healing and helping others manage their everyday stress and she shares how she applies it: "When we learn about how trauma impacts our minds and bodies, we are more compassionate with ourselves and others. When we are curious about what causes pain and grief, we can help to create connection and ceremony for healing. Healing happens when our mind, body, and spirit are connected and when we are in relationship to others in our community."[3]

Asking for help is a tool to add to your life toolbox. Stuff happens to us that we don't expect, and having the courage to ask for help when we need it should be something we are okay doing. In Dr. John Deloney's book, *Building a Non-Anxious Life,* he states, "..there's a difference between choosing to be healed –past tense – and choosing healing as a life direction in the present and future."[4] For many people, it is a combination. We need to be healed, and we need to make choices consistently so we are in a better place and stop the cycles that hurt our children.

Thought to Carry with You

"When you reach the end of your life, do you want to be one of the people who are glad they did, or one of the people who wish they had? Start doing the things today that will matter tomorrow. Don't leave this world without giving it your all. The best inheritance you can leave your kids is an example of how to live a full and meaningful life. Live your life so that your children can tell their children that you not only stood for something wonderful – you acted on it!" - Dan Zadra, *Where Will You Be Five Years From Today?*

JOURNAL PROMPTS

1. Have you paused to be honest with yourself and how you are feeling? How are your relationships with your family, friends, and co-workers?

_____

_____

_____

_____

_____

_____

_____

_____

_____

_____

_____

_____

_____

_____

_____

_____

_____

_____

2. How have you been feeling lately? Are there any red flags when you answer that question honestly? Have you been taking care of your body? Are you sleeping and eating right? Do you move every day?

_____

_____

_____

_____

_____

_____

_____

_____

_____

_____

_____

_____

_____

_____

_____

_____

3. Are there ways you could be more compassionate with yourself and others? Be curious with yourself. Why do you do some of the things you do?

_____

_____

_____

_____

_____

_____

_____

_____

_____

_____

_____

_____

_____

_____

_____

_____

_____

_____

Resources

After reading this, perhaps you have realized that you or someone you love could also use some help. Below, you find a list of places that can direct you in the right direction. I wish I had read more about mental health and options before I was in a crisis with someone. I would have made a different choice in the response option I took. Being informed is never a bad thing.

Crisis? Please call or text 988 to talk to someone 24/7

- Reach out to your healthcare provider
- The National Council for Mental Wellbeing offers a search feature to help you locate organizations that are committed to providing mental health services, usually without regard to whether the person can pay for the services or not https://www.thenationalcouncil.org/
- NAMI (National Alliance on Mental Illness) Helpline is 1-800-950-6264. You can also find resources and support at https://www.nami.org/
- National Institute of Mental Health offers research and resources at https://www.nimh.nih.gov/
- A general informational resource is SAMHSA (Substance Abuse and Mental Health Services Administration. https://www.samhsa.gov/find-help/national-helpline   or 1-800-662-4357
- Information on the different types of miscarriages and the help you may need: https://www.tommys.org/baby-loss-support/miscarriage-information-and-support/types-of-miscarriage

Chapter 5

THE NEIGHBORS

The expression on my friend's face was priceless. She kept saying, "No way!" as we walked, and I continued to tell my story. It sounded like something out of the movies, but it wasn't. It was real and painful. I was glad to be able to be on the other side of the story, making jokes and feeling the relief that my body needed so badly. As we went through everything, I realized we weren't just stressed; we were overwhelmed. As Brené Brown describes in *Atlas of the Heart*, "If stress is being in the weeds. Overwhelmed is being blown."[1] Some situations create a deadly current underneath our everyday life–a current that we try to navigate but that slowly pulls us under.

In the early spring of 1998, my husband and I decided that we needed to move closer to the main road system for better access to medical care. It would also make it easier for my husband to commute to his job on the North Slope of Alaska by having better access to the airport. Finding land and securing it so we could begin clearing and building our home was a juggling process; we were in the middle of selling our Fairbanks home, but we also needed to be out of our cabin in Eureka. Fortunately, we were able to work out an agreement that allowed us to start cutting trees and clearing brush for the long driveway that would need to be put in place on the property north of Healy, Alaska.

We began relocating, driving five to six hours one way, unloading, and always needing to return to care for the dogs still in Eureka. I hit a wall of exhaustion around 11:00 p.m. after unloading items at the new property north of Healy. I had decided to pull over at the end of the road at our property and nap while the girls slept in the back of the truck before heading back to Eureka. I quickly fell into a deep sleep when I was startled awake by a rapping on my truck window. On the other side was a man's scarred and unshaven face staring directly at me. The haunting laughter that followed scared me and unnerved me. I had to take a minute to breathe but panicked about what to do.

"What are you doing here?" he jeered.

"I needed some sleep before I drove back. We purchased the property back there and are in the process of moving." I responded.

I could tell he meant to intimidate me and was carrying a gun. I was doing my best to stay in control, but I was terrified. He saw I had the kids in the back of the truck and backed away from the window slightly. He explained that he and his girlfriend lived in the cabin up the road. They liked to know who was on the road and kept track of who was coming and going. I explained that I would be leaving soon but would be back. He nodded and left. Even though I was still exhausted, I was too scared to sleep any more. I waited a few minutes but decided to use the adrenaline rush to drive and get as far as possible. Maybe I could find a safe place to rest along the way. One thing I knew was that I was not looking forward to interacting with our closest neighbors.

We learned that the land owners had given the woman, a single mom with two children, the opportunity to stay in the cabin that adjoined the property we were purchasing. The boyfriend showed up after they agreed to rent it to her. I knew I needed to keep an open mind about the neighbors, but I got a bad feeling every time I saw him. I didn't particularly appreciate how he looked at me like he was planning what he could do. I had an icky feeling.

While we worked on the road, we stayed in a camping tent where I used piles of clothes and blankets to build a safe place for the kids. Our youngest daughter was just beginning to walk. The tent was located just below the hill from the neighbor's cabin. I hated the feeling that we were constantly being watched. I was relieved when we could drive to the top of the road, where my husband had built a platform and set up a wall tent. We could stay dry, store a few things, and have a place to sleep. I was looking for flexible work, and one of the local tour companies needed their vans cleaned every evening. We purchased a portable generator and power washer so I could clean the vans after the girls went to bed. We hauled the water we needed in a large tank. I felt like every time I left and returned, I was being watched.

One day, I left to go into town with the girls and left my husband to work on the property. He was working hard to get pads built for the kennel and cabin. There was so much work to do. He realized he needed fuel and had left to drive to Healy to get some. Shortly after he returned, he discovered someone had come to the property and stolen our portable generator, chain saw, brush cutter, and several other items. He hadn't been gone long. Someone had been watching to know when he left. My husband went to the

63

neighbors asking if they had seen anyone, and they said no, but they understood there were trails around that locals might have used. The police informed us that we could file the report but that the penalty for anyone they caught would be fairly mild because it was not locked up in a structure. Unfortunately, I could not keep the job cleaning tour vans, as we no longer had the equipment needed.

I created flyers that we posted around the local area. Thankfully, one kind and honest individual eventually let us and the authorities know he had purchased one of the items from a local young guy. The young man was struggling with drugs, and everyone assumed he needed funds for his habit. Unfortunately, they were never able to recover the other items.

Only a few days later, my husband found one of our blue heelers had been killed. She was tiny in size for a heeler but mighty, and she was the one that would let you know if someone was near that shouldn't be. She was protective but also had a pretty good read on people and usually understood if they were friends or foes. I thought she felt like I did about the neighbor's live-in boyfriend. I continued to feel watched, and although the neighbors once again denied any knowledge of her death, I couldn't believe them watching the road and yet knowing nothing about what had happened.

Anyone who has had things stolen understands how violated you feel. We knew some of the neighbors who lived a few miles away, and they had been a great help with labor and resources. They also attended one of the local churches and arranged for their men's group to help us get a shed constructed so we had somewhere to store equipment that could be locked. We also purchased a large canvas hoop tent that would allow us to store most of our belongings, stay dry, and have space for sleeping and cook-ing. The door on it could be locked as well. Once the cabin was completed, we could use it for other storage. I hated feeling like someone might steal things from us. I was reaching a point where I was almost afraid to sleep. I took comfort in the fact that at least the sled dogs would bark if someone or wildlife were around. Then, my husband left for a shift on the north slope.

Exhaustion was a regular visitor, and I was thankful when the sleep overtook me. I awoke, startled by the screams coming through the woods. Alarms were going off in my body. Panic was hitting me full-on. I was alone with my two little girls, and there was no reliable communication. There was only a canvas tent sep-arating us from the world. That was when I heard the gunshots. Out in the wilderness with the beginnings of our modest cabin, the girls and I were asleep in our tent when the neighbors through the woods began fighting. The screams and the gunshots seemed to come closer. I quickly grabbed my sleeping three-year-old and one-year-old and tucked them down underneath me and my heavy sleeping bag, praying that my body would shield them and that someone would find them if the bullets struck me.

During a lull in the fighting, I called the land owner on our bag cell phone. To contact anyone, I had to leave the tent and get reception. I explained what was happening but wasn't sure what to do. My husband was away, and I was afraid. I was worried for the woman. It sounded like he was hitting her, but it was hard to know. I needed to return to the children, which meant I could not call the police and stay on hold for information. I would leave it to him to make the call. I repositioned where we were sleeping, thinking it would be harder for a bullet to get to us. I don't think I slept at all that night.

I remember calling my husband and telling him I was unsure if I could do this anymore. We had everything invested into that property, and it wasn't like I could pick up the sled dogs and stay somewhere else. I was going to have to figure something out. I was in the middle of getting chores done when the neighbor appeared through the woods. She had bruises on her face and arm. She was quiet but spoke very clearly: "I don't know who called the cops on my man, but if it happens again, I will have to come take care of the person who did." I quietly responded, "Okay." She left.

I went to the tent and fell to the floor, crying out to God that I couldn't take this constant fear and stress anymore – it was just too much. "Please, help me!" I cried out. After collecting myself and leaving for work, I remember calling my husband to tell him what had happened. I was on edge, and I hated feeling like every alarm in my body was ready to go off. I remember calling my mother, crying, and telling her I felt like a failure, but could she come to get the girls to let them stay with them? I needed to know they were safe and could be normal little kids. I was crushed at the thought of not being with them, as they were my world, but I needed to know they were safe. Once we got the cabin enclosed, I would come to get them. It also meant I would have time to look for a better-paying job.

Later that evening, as I was preparing supper on the camp stove, I heard a vehicle. I eyed where I had put my rifle and went to look to see who was there. The landowner was bringing a small camper he had and parking it near the tent. He then explained that I should go about my regular business but that he would spend the night in the trailer and be here in case of a problem. I finally let myself sleep. He spent a night or two, and then a few men from the church took turns staying the night, allowing me a few precious nights of sleep.

Because the neighbors kept track of who was coming and going, nothing happened while others were there. A few nights after the men stopped spending the night, the arguing started again, but thankfully, I never heard the gunfire. The constant fear and lack of sleep took a toll on my husband and me. While the girls were gone, we worked until the wee hours of the morning and would be back up a few hours later. Summer turned rainy, making progress slow.

One afternoon, a state trooper appeared in my driveway. He had stopped by to check on me. He asked if I knew how to shoot. I explained that I was comfortable with a rifle. "Have you ever thought about what you would do in a self-defense situation?" he asked. "No," I responded, wondering where this was leading. He told me he was instructed not to respond to calls on our neighbor without a backup. Without going into details, he explained that there had been some other police altercations involving the boyfriend. Currently, the closest backup was over 1 ½ hours away. They might not be able to get here in time to save us, so he wanted to be sure we were mentally prepared. If I wasn't already tense, this was adding to it.

Fall was coming, so we had plenty to do. The girls were back home after staying with my mom. The cabin was enclosed, but we didn't have heat yet. The girls and I had been out in our driveway getting ready to do some chores. I was carrying our youngest in a backpack while our three-year-old was running ahead with our blue heeler close behind; as we rounded the bend to the side of the driveway behind the neighbor's place, my eye caught movement. It was a pack of dogs belonging to the neighbors, the leader lunging toward our three-year-old. I remember screaming and the blue heeler intercepting the lead dog, giving me enough time to swoop up my daughter and get her away from the dogs. I was terrified for ourselves and our pet dog. I started yelling at the pack leader, trying to keep the other dogs from joining in. My hands were full, and I knew the girls were scared. I kicked some rocks from the ground, trying to distract them and yell at them to go. With my heart pounding in my chest, our heeler backed up close to me; after a moment, I repeated my request for them to go, and thankfully, they left. I was still shaking a few hours later when my husband returned from the fish wheel and moose hunting. My husband called the troopers that night to add to the growing list of interactions the neighbors were having with the troopers. I worried it was only adding to their hatred of us.

We focused on the cabin, and my husband worked tirelessly to prepare it for winter. I had started a new job where I worked long hours. The girls were settling into daycare when they weren't with their dad. The weather turned cold, and we still had no heat. My husband developed pneumonia, and we had dogs to care for as well. Upon learning of our situation, friends generously let us spend a few nights at their house so my husband could get strong enough to work on the house and care for the dogs. Of course, we worried what the neighbors might do while we were gone. It seemed like an ever-present stressor.

Feeding the dogs meant building a fire for the barrel dog pot and cooking a large drum of fish and rice to add to the dry food. The fire had to be maintained so it didn't get too hot, but it did not go out. We needed the wood we had cut for the dog pot and the wood stoves. While a friend was staying with us, she observed the neighbors helping themselves to some firewood on our property.

Right or wrong, we decided not to confront them until we could determine it was happening regularly or caught them ourselves.

It was cold that winter, with lots of -30F to -40F days and nights. We had no electricity, so we would have to wake up every few hours to start the truck so I could get to work the following day. My husband juggled training and caring for the dogs while I juggled working full-time, the kids, and living in an unfinished cabin without electricity and running water.

One evening, while my husband was away racing, I was home with the girls and a dear friend helping me while my husband was away. It was getting dark, and we saw a friend from a few miles away pull up in their car without the lights on. I called out a greeting to him, and he told me to be quiet. I was immediately confused. Once in the cabin, he explained that he would take us to their house. A Special Weapons and Tactics (SWAT) team was at the bottom of the driveway, waiting to move in on our closest neighbor's house through the woods. I was beginning to think that my first impression of the neighbor's boyfriend was valid.

The landowner called us while we were out of town to let us know that neighbors were trying to claim harassment from the police and the landowner. He informed us that he had a private investigator look into the boyfriend, who had over 90 recorded charges or incidents with the law. The guy was officially bad news, but there was nothing we could do about it. He had to honor their rental agreement as long as their rent payments were current. I tried to tell myself everything would be okay. Somehow, my body knew I was lying.

A few weeks later, we received another call from the landowner telling us the neighbors were gone. They discovered the boyfriend had been arrested and would be in custody for a while, and apparently, the mom and kids decided to head back to a western state where she had family. Both my husband and I slept hard that night. We had not realized the amount of overwhelm we were dealing with until it was released.

Reflecting on the year, we realized we had argued and were often sick and exhausted – all signals that, whether real or perceived, we were suffering from chronic stress, never knowing whether we were safe and being watched. Stress creates an imbalance in our bodies, and over time, it impacts our body's ability to cope. Our individual perceptions of the stressful situation may have differed, but "the more perceived demands outweigh a person's coping capacity, the more severe stress becomes."[2] It took its toll on us as a family. We were simply trying to get through our day to get our family to a better place. We had nowhere else to go, so we kept pushing through while the waters of overwhelm grew around us.

In reflecting, I realized how important it was to accept the help of friends and family. I didn't want to "impose" on anyone or make extra work for them. I hated "bothering" people, but we needed them. Community and connection are so important. I needed sleep and rest. I was not able to refill my already empty energy cells. I was like a cell phone that could only get a 10 percent battery charge; I was functioning but was always on the verge of losing all my charge.

Community is important, as we cannot heal or thrive in isolation. We heal in community. We were meant for community, and each culture has built traditions around community, such as ceremonies and celebrations. Back in the 1970s, Dr. Bruce Alexander conducted an experiment with rats. Researchers had already shown that a rat given the choice of water or water laced with heroin or cocaine would drink the laced water until the rat overdosed and died. Dr. Alexander replicated the study but instead of a single rat, he created a community of rats where they were free to roam and play, but had the same choices of water or laced water. These rats preferred the plain water, and if they did happen to drink the laced water, none of them drank it in excess to the point of death.[3] Our other neighbors, friends, and family help keep us safe. We need them to feel safe.

If you find yourself feeling on edge and exhausted all the time, take the time to examine your life. Be honest with yourself by looking at your environment, relationships, and mental health. Reach out to family and friends; don't try to go on this journey alone. We were made to have people in our lives, not just electronic versions of people. Decide to embrace mindfulness, commit to being fully present, and cultivate curiosity while disregarding internal distractions. It helps if you are willing to change how you talk to yourself and others. You will also need to be sure you are taking care of your health by making wise food choices and getting some exercise.

Chapters in our lives can sometimes feel like they are straight out of a television show or just the same routine day after day. However, we must remember that life is not a practice session; we only have one chance to go through it. Decide you will make the most of the ride by caring for yourself and those around you while being a part of a larger community.

Thought to Carry with You

"You need to take care of yourself to take care of others…
You can't say you're going to do a mission if you don't have
a mission for yourself first."
– Andre Rush, Army veteran and
former White House Chef

JOURNAL PROMPTS

1. Do you have a stressful situation that is turning into overwhelm? Have you thought about the people in your daily life? Do they bring you joy and lift you up when you need it? Would they be there for you in the middle of the night if needed? We all need friends who will be there if something happens.

_____

_____

_____

_____

_____

_____

_____

_____

_____

_____

_____

_____

_____

_____

_____

_____

2. Have you thought about the long-term effects of something that is bothering you? If so, write down what is bothering you. Have you noticed any health issues related to the constant stress?

_____

_____

_____

_____

_____

_____

_____

_____

_____

_____

_____

_____

_____

_____

_____

_____

_____

_____

3. Would you go if a friend or family member needed you in the middle of the night? What kinds of things would you go for, and what types of things would you not go for in the middle of the night?

_____

_____

_____

_____

_____

_____

_____

_____

_____

_____

_____

_____

_____

_____

_____

_____

_____

_____

_____

Resources

Two of my favorite books written in everyday language that help me think things through and keep perspective are below.

1. *Building a Non-Anxious Life* by Dr. John Delony
2. *Atlas of the Heart* by Dr. Brené Brown

Chapter 6

THE BABY

T he medical chart read, "Five pregnancies, two live births." Five words. One single line out of pages and pages of my medical chart made my knees buckle and my stomach churn. I thought I had dealt with the grief and walked through the pain, but those words brought a flood of memories and heartache. We had been through so much over the past several years. I wasn't trying to answer the "why" anymore. I was trying to move forward by focusing on how to move forward and where we wanted to head. I rested my hand on my now protruding belly, praying this little guy would make it and complete our family. All my children were blessings, but this one was bringing light after so much darkness.

I closed my eyes as the flood of memories came rushing back. We were still living north of Healy, but by 2006, we had expanded the cabin and had running water and electricity. Our girls were now nine and eleven, with our eldest turning twelve soon. They attended the local school and participated in sports, church, and community activities. The Healy community had embraced us and our children. My husband and I were busy running and managing our sled dog racing kennel and building a tourism business. The days were packed with more than we could do in the day, but we were blessed with a great community and friends. An entry from my journal during that time period reflected where I was at with life:

> *I must find time to write more often – so much to catch up on, but I am exhausted and must get up early in the morning to water, feed, and clean dogs before my online vet class starts. The biggest news is that I think I am a few months pregnant. I did a home pregnancy test, and it was positive, but I have not followed up with a doctor's visit yet. I know I should because of my age. I am sure to be added to the high-risk category….*

I had a mix of emotions – excited but scared. I was helping my husband hook the dog team up. He was about to go on a training run, and he was telling me what needed to get done that day. I was asking him if he wanted any more children. He responded, telling me he wasn't opposed to it but wasn't sure we could handle any more. He stopped mid-stride and turned to me. "Why? Why are you asking me that question?" I tried to read his face before responding: "Because I think I am pregnant." I found myself journaling through this journey and had the following entry:

> *Life is at such an out-of-control pace. I am determined to slow it down, but I know it is going to get crazier before it gets calmer. I want to get several things done or caught up before the baby. Yes! I am definitely pregnant. I went for a blood test to confirm it. We kept the news entirely to ourselves until a few days ago when I had to ask one of my best*

friends to help with some medical forms... I want to see the doctor before we start telling other people.

I was concerned about the logistics of all we had in front of me, and my parents were dealing with some medical issues. I wanted to talk to my mom before we told others so I could discuss the summer for the girls and possibly a visit to them. I was sure my family would want to meet the baby, and the girls would not want to be away from the new baby for very long. I was working through my thoughts in my journal:

> *... Before we tell my mother-in-law, maybe we should tell the girls but ask them not to say anything until after we have told all their grandparents, aunts, and uncles. I need to get some sleep. I know so much of what I have written is babble, but after telling my best friend and talking about it with someone besides my husband, the reality is sinking in, and I had better get things done. I miss my husband. He is away training, and when we don't argue, I miss him. Our eldest daughter is training with him. I hope she is having fun. I love my daughters so very much. It was a nice day with my youngest daughter. She is so easy-going – well, most of the time. I need to get a lot done, and I have been pretty sick. I am going to try to get eight hours of sleep!*

Only a few days later, I had another journal entry.

> *Okay, things did not go as planned. We have made it into 2007; I hope this is not a sign of how the year is going to go. Last night, my mother-in-law was in the living room, wanting to know what I was going to do with one of the little coats I had been sorting through. I had been sorting through hats, mittens, scarves, etc., cleaning, and I had set aside one*

of the smaller parkas to clean and put away. She picked it up and wanted to know why I was keeping it. I replied I was saving it for the future. She wanted to know what for – she can be demanding when she wants to be (and they wonder where my husband gets that personality trait?). I looked at my husband to give me some help. My mother-in-law was not going to stop until I gave an acceptable answer. After a moment of silence, my husband says, "Just tell her." To which she responds, "Tell me what?" I lower my voice and quietly say, "Please don't say anything, but we are expecting another one, so I want to keep the coat for the future." The look on her face was disbelief. I do believe it was one of the few times in my life I might have left her speechless. I walked out of the room, upset because I had not wanted to tell her yet and worried that the girls had overheard us.

I got busy with the things that needed to be done. My mother-in-law came to say she was sorry, but she just didn't expect that response from us. She asked if I had been to the doctor. I told her I had been to confirm the pregnancy, but we had not told anyone yet because we still had paperwork to complete to figure out where I wanted to be seen. Using the dates, I should be about four months along. The conversation ended abruptly as our eldest daughter was coming into the room. I had wanted my mom to be the first to know, but sometimes things don't go as planned, and that's okay... I decided to call my mom in the morning, and then we would let the girls know. I have lots of chores to do, bills to pay, and errands to run. I had better get some sleep.

The days went by quickly, and the to-do list was longer than the day. I was struggling with thoughts about a friend whom I felt

I needed to reach out to, and I filled several pages of my journal, trying to figure out what to do. The situation weighed heavy on me, but we had so much to do I was trying not to dwell on it. I did, however, tell my mom and the girls I was expecting and wrote about it in my journal:

> *Everyone was excited. I wasn't going to say anything to anyone else, but my mom pointed out that it is okay to tell friends, especially close ones, because if something does happen, they can be there for you. So I told our two other close friends. I asked the girls to wait to tell their friends for a few days. I have developed a cold that I can't seem to shake.*

Life continued to be busy with the kids' activities and everything that happens during the busy racing season. A few weeks later, something didn't feel right. I took to my journal to write out my thoughts:

> *Baby,*
>
> *I am afraid of losing you. I have given you to God and asked that we be given the privilege of raising you. A few days ago, you started to worry me. I have had some dark, bloody discharge. Things don't seem right. The cramps are reminding me of the last miscarriage, but they seem to have subsided.*

I added an entry a few hours later –

> *Oh baby, I think I lost you – that was too much blood... I hope I am wrong.*

The next day, I drove a few hours to town to see the doctor. I could tell something was wrong when the ultrasound technician would not look me in the eye and would only tell me that the doctor would talk to me. I must have known I would need help processing because I brought my journal with me to town.

Dear Baby,

You are in God's hands – you always have been. I was just hoping to have the chance to hold you and love you through our life here. I realize there is a chance I might not get that opportunity since we did not hear your heartbeat a little bit ago, but we are going to have an ultrasound. We are praying you were hiding out on the Doppler, but we will have to see. I keep hoping you are playing games with us. I know you are still inside me despite the bleeding. It's just whether you are growing or have gone to be with Jesus. I love you.

A few hours later...

Dear Baby,

I know for sure now you are with Jesus. I know He will care for you, and I will be with you someday. I am mourning not having the chance to hold you and be with you, but I have to trust that Jesus will help me understand. What am I going to do now? I have to go back to the doctor tomorrow to help get what's left of you out of my body and check to be sure everything is okay. I'd be lying if I didn't say I was struggling. I am. I love you. I can't believe I am writing goodbye.

A few hours later...

Things have not been easy. Your daddy cried, too. Your sisters did, too. Everyone is so sad. Your daddy was really ready to be there for you. The neighbors have been really nice. They helped out, and my best friend is driving me back to town for the procedure. It sounds awful, and I wish I was having you in four months instead.

The next day, things just got darker.

It has been a long day. Words cannot describe the feelings I had while I sat at the clinic waiting for the doctor to come. I was so overcome with grief and dread. The doctor came in, and we talked about several things. I wanted to make sure this wasn't a repeat kind of situation. I didn't understand, but the fact that we have two healthy children and are healthy means we should be okay. The procedure was awful but not as bad as I think it could have been. I felt pain, but it wasn't for long periods of time. The tissue sample was so blood-tinged. I will say it was challenging to walk it to the lab for the pathology because when I got there, the lady needing the paperwork yanked the sample from my hands, and it hit the floor. I was fighting tears as I scooped it up from the floor. I think they thought it was just urine. They were so insensitive. I was so devastated. I wanted to cry. I hope everything worked out for them to test the tissue. The doctor was very reassuring about everything, which made it easier to deal with. I think I hit rock bottom before the procedure and feel like I am heading in the right direction.

I know folks are praying for me, and that helps. I worry about my husband and need to ask God to please be with him and help him do well in the race. I love him so much more as I saw the sensitive, caring side of him that I needed to see and feel.

Everyone knew, and the pain was not just mine to carry. Our girls and extended family had been so excited about the baby. Our youngest daughter had been practicing caring for her future sibling with her baby dolls. After the initial dose of reality that after nine years, I would be a mom again, I had allowed myself to look forward to another baby. Now, I had suffered a miscarriage at five months. I was sitting in my grief, not wanting to share it with everyone else. The sheer hurt in my little girl's eyes, when we told her the baby had died, shattered what was left of my heart. I knew I would need to walk with my family through the grief, not just myself.

We were so busy it was easy to bury the grief in busyness. Everyone dealt with it differently. I did not understand how differently children process death, depending on where they are developmentally. Both girls could have used more patience and a listening ear from me to help them walk through the grief. I didn't expect the occasional lashouts that accompanied the anger they were processing. Thankfully, our neighbor and one of our female employees both offered listening ears and answered difficult questions for them.

I had to learn that grief looked different for everyone in my family. Grief is messy, and the process may not be as linear as once was thought. Brené Brown says there are three foundational elements to grief: loss, longing, and feeling lost. The loss isn't just about the separation due to death; it's the loss of what was normal, the future, and even what we thought or understood about the person. Longing, Brown explains, "is not conscious wanting; it's an involuntary yearning for wholeness, for understanding, for meaning, for the opportunity to regain or even simply touch what we've lost." Feeling lost comes into play when we recognize that grief requires one to "reorient every part of our physical, emotional, and social worlds."[1] We all need connection and a place to safely tell our story. I am forever grateful for the friends and family that rallied for our girls when I could not.

I also learned that I was a part of a much larger club than I realized. Because people in the community knew, I was amazed at the number of women who would stop and tell me how sorry they were, and many would add their own experiences to the conversation. For so long, miscarriage felt like a "dirty" secret that no one spoke of. I was learning that the community of women and connection were a part of the healing. When the women confided in me, I could ask questions and learn from their experiences.

My grief was so confusing to me at times. No one mentioned that I would be dealing with postpartum hormones and that my body would be out of sync for a bit while I recovered. You are dealing with birth and death all at the same time. A few close friends checked in regularly but gave me space when I needed. I found solace in nature and clung to my faith as I walked through the grieving. I journaled, and I stayed busy. Author Adriel Booker, who wrote the book *Grace Like Scarlett: Grieving Hope after Miscarriage and Loss,* shares tips on her website on how you can help and care for a friend that has gone through a miscarriage or stillbirth:[2]

1. Don't be silent
2. Be available to listen and talk… or not
3. Give permission to feel whatever she is feeling (help if it appears serious, like deep depression)
4. Refrain from offering pat answers or religious cliches
5. Offer practical help
6. Don't assume that someone else is looking after them
7. If you are a person of faith, pray
8. Don't forget dad

9. Try to understand her triggers
10. Call her baby by name
11. Engage in her story
12. Give her a thoughtful gift or care package
13. Mark your calendar for the important milestones
14. Be sensitive about "trying again" and future pregnancies

Thankfully, we have entered a time when the internet has connected people and resources that were not as readily available to me. I have included several websites and books in the resources of this chapter to help you navigate a difficult season like this if you should ever need it. Just know that as dark as this time can feel, the light does return. Our family was blessed with the birth of a healthy baby boy in the spring of 2008. Your story may end differently but know there is help reaching the light if you can't get there on your own.

Thought to Carry with You

"Children are always the only future the human race has; teach them well." – Unknown

JOURNAL PROMPTS

1. Have you lost a baby? Do you have a support system around you? Were you able to grieve? Have you considered writing a letter to your baby? Do you have someone you can talk to about your loss? Think about who you can connect with that might help you as you walk through this difficult time or memory.

_____

_____

_____

_____

_____

_____

_____

_____

_____

_____

_____

_____

_____

_____

2. When you think of children, what thoughts come to mind when you think of the different stages – infancy, toddler, pre-K, elementary, middle school, and high school?

_____

_____

_____

_____

_____

_____

_____

_____

_____

_____

_____

_____

_____

_____

_____

_____

_____

_____

_____

3. If you have lost a baby, walk through the day you lost the baby. What were you wearing? Where were you at? What time of the year was it? Who was with you? What did you do that day? Be willing to use all your senses as you walk through the day. Don't forget to remind yourself how loved you are. Reach out if you need help processing it.

_____

_____

_____

_____

_____

_____

_____

_____

_____

_____

_____

_____

_____

_____

_____

_____

_____

_____

4. Do you know of someone that has gone through a miscarriage or stillbirth? How might you look at their experience differently after reading this chapter? Have you considered how you might help the person you know or how you might help if someone in the future goes through this?

_____

_____

_____

_____

_____

_____

_____

_____

_____

_____

_____

_____

_____

_____

_____

_____

_____

_____

Resources

Current thoughts on how to help heal from losing a baby include finding a support group, addressing your grief and understanding the grief journey, having a place to share your story, and journaling. Please use the following resources as a place to help you as you walk this journey. Don't forget that Dad needs help too. Some of these resources also have excellent information to help the grieving dad.

- Adriel Booker, whose book *Grace Like Scarlett: Grieving Hope after Miscarriage and Loss,* offers a community support group, Our Scarlett Stories. You can find her story and resources at https://adrielbooker.com/grace-like-scarlett/.

- Author Diane Newcomer has a website that addresses topics like infertility, miscarriage, grief, and suffering. You can find her at https://dianenewcomer.com/.

- The National Institute of Health (NIH) has a grief and support page with several resources listed, and an article out of Europe has eight suggestions of things to do after having a miscarriage https://www.nct.org.uk/pregnancy/miscarriage/miscarriage-eight-things-can-help-afterwards

- Author Jenny Albers wrote *Courageously Expecting*, addressing pregnancy after loss, and can be found here: https://jennyalbers.com/courageously-expecting/

- Dr. Rachelle Keng addresses the anxiety that can surround a woman during and right after pregnancy in her book *Woven in the Womb*. You can order her book and find resources at https://www.rachellekeng.com/.

Chapter 7

THE SCHOOL
ASSEMBLY

Sometimes, we want to help people who are not ready to be helped. We can cause more harm than good by forcing conversations the other person is unprepared to have. Forcing someone to unpack trauma for which they are not ready is akin to asking someone to give you directions to a place they don't know how to reach. They are already lost, and you want them to help you with directions? As absurd as that sounds, that is what we are doing. We mean well, as we want everyone to be where they are intended to be and be happy, but it is not that simple with folks not ready for the journey. I learned this lesson the hard way.

Sheer panic ran through me as I repeatedly listened to the message. "What on earth could this be about?" My mind raced as I tried calling the phone number, but I was only directed to a messaging system. Why would a detective from the state troopers be calling me? His recording mentioned he was with the child investigation unit. What could it possibly be? Our young son was with his grandparents when he wasn't with us. The girls were teenagers and challenging at times, but I could think of nothing that would warrant police involvement. Panic struck as I recalled a story of a family losing their children after being falsely accused of child abuse. I was shaking. I don't know what I would do without my children. "Oh God, please help!" I called out. I wasn't even sure what I was facing. I just knew there were bad people out there. I tried calling the number again, but there was only a message. It was a Friday evening after 5 PM. I tried calling the main information number to be informed that the detective would not be on shift again until Monday. I didn't know if my heart would make it until Monday.

We had moved to Fairbanks the year before. The girls were both in high school, and our youngest daughter was a freshman at the local high school. Our son had not started school yet. I called my husband, who was working, and asked if he knew what was going on. He appeared as clueless as me. I shared my fear that someone had made something up about us. I was scared that we would lose our children, but I didn't know what it could be over. I was far from a perfect parent, but I loved my children and would not hesitate to lay my life down for any of them. I could tell he was worried, too, and we were so confused.

My mind was racing to make sense of things, and my body's alarms were going off. I was looking for anything to help it make sense. I remembered one of the girls telling me when we first moved to town that they had learned you could turn your parents in for abuse, and they had heard stories about kids doing that to get away from their parents. I remember explaining how it was a good thing if the kids who turned their parents in were being abused, but if they had lied, they might end up in a scarier situation in state custody. I had made a lot of mistakes in parenting; however, I tried to be honest and have open discussions with them – even the hard ones.

I needed to know what was going on. I started with our oldest daughter, asking if she had talked to anyone or accused her dad or me of doing anything. "No," she responded emphatically. I explained that I had a message left by a detective and I needed to know if she knew anything. Could she think of anyone to whom she talked to and said anything? Once again, she answered firmly, "No." That was when I heard my younger daughter quietly say with tears in her eyes, "It was me."

"What?" I said as I looked at her, making herself small on the bed. I was shocked and worried.

"I'm sorry. I am so sorry. There was an assembly at school, and they broke us up into small groups and asked us questions. They had everyone close their eyes after asking some questions and then asked, 'If one of these things has happened to you, raise your hand.' And so I did." She responded. She explained how she got called to the counselor's room later and asked to tell her story. She went on about how she didn't want people to know, but she had just raised her hand honestly, not thinking anything would happen. The counselor then reported the conversation to the state police, and she was pretty sure that was why they were calling.

From there, she and I had a tearful and painful conversation about what had happened. I let her share her story and cry. I was in shock, but I hugged and cried with her. I reassured her how much I loved her and how sorry I was she had carried this inside her. I told her she did not need to walk through this pain alone.

We would try to figure things out together. Nothing had prepared me for the conversation. She shared how there had been an incident while she was with friends. The specifics of what happened involve others who were minors at the time. Since it is her story to unpack instead of mine, which I respect, I hope those who know her will also respect that and not ask her about it.

After leaving her room, I went to my bedroom and into our bathroom with the doors closed. I needed to be as far away from the kids as I could. I found myself in anguish, leaning against the door and slowly falling into a heap on the floor. Words could not be formed, only cries and sounds I didn't recognize as my own. Brené Brown describes what I was feeling: "Anguish not only takes away our ability to breathe, feel, and think – it comes for our bones. Anguish often causes us to physically crumple in on ourselves, literally bringing us to our knees or forcing us all the way to the ground. The element of powerlessness is what makes anguish traumatic. We are unable to change, reverse, or negotiate what has happened."[1]

I thought I had done everything right. I had ensured I knew where my kids were. I knew who was with them and watching them. How could this have happened to my child? I couldn't decide whether I wanted to cry or scream in anger. I did what I thought a good parent should do and tried to "fix" it.

I learned how to find a counselor in our town, and I soon discovered we lacked counselors for teenagers in our community. I didn't want anyone to know, so I went through my employer's assistance program to find someone to whom she could talk. Once I found a provider in the network, I would make appointments, and I hoped this would help. I didn't recognize soon enough that my daughter was going to the counseling visits because she thought that was what I wanted her to do. It was, but it was because I wanted it to help her and "fix" things. She obviously wasn't enjoying the sessions, and I found her getting angry at me. So I tried another counselor and another one, hoping our daughter would connect with someone to help her. Finally, the last counselor looked me in the eye and said, "You can't fix this. Your daughter is not ready to deal with the trauma. Not only is she dealing with what happened, but she has been asked to relive it. She did not choose any of this. She did not choose this time to disclose it – the school did. My advice for you is to be there for her and when she is ready, walk beside her. This is her trauma to heal, not yours. Yours is different than hers."

I remember letting her words sink in and realizing that we were adding more trauma for her to have to deal with at some point. Trauma was a new "buzz" word at the time, but I was learning firsthand what it meant. I was dealing with the fact that no matter how badly I wanted to "fix" things, I couldn't. I had been angry at the school for thinking they were helping teenagers by having assemblies like this. Who decided these things? A quick internet search revealed that although there were some life-changing assemblies out there, there were a lot of bad experiences out there as well. I needed to let my anger and frustration go. Maybe I needed to shift my focus to healing and wellness. In the book *Indigenous Knowledge and Mental Health,* LaVerne Xilegg Demientieff and Patrick Frank point out in their chapter, "I Remember Who I am: Deg Xit'an Athabascan Perspective on Wellness," that "You cannot heal by fighting off grief and trauma with anger or with negative thoughts or force; you have to do this with love, compassion, and forgiveness in relation to all things."[2]

Our daughter would, in time, be ready to get the help she needed. I also sought help to figure out how to help her. I think both of us learned some difficult lessons. I needed to work on myself and change some of the inner stories I told myself to be more aware and stronger for my daughter. I had to let my daughter go on her own journey of healing, but I needed her to know that we loved her and we were there for her – no matter what. I started looking for tools and ways I could help those around me.

One tool I added to my toolbox was from a Mental Health First Aid course. The training uses the acronym ALGEE:

- A = Approach/Assess
- L= Listen Non-judgmentally
- G= Give Reassurance and information
- E= Encourage Professional Help
- E= Encourage Self Help and Support

If we notice something that seems off about a friend or family member, we must let them know that we are there for them if they need anyone. Paying attention to their verbal and nonverbal cues is essential, and remember to consider culture. For example, I have had students from cultures where eye contact is not the norm, so it would not be a sign that something is wrong if they didn't make eye contact with me.

We also send a message when we remember details about our conversations with people. It is a way to show you that you listened and cared. Sometimes, sitting silently with someone is the most powerful thing you can do. Somewhere over the years, I heard a pastor share how, as a young guy fresh out of seminary, he would go to be with people after a tragedy and felt he needed to pray and share words of wisdom. A few months into his job, an Indigenous Elder invited the young pastor to his home. The Elder greeted him at the door and asked him to come sit, and then the Elder remained quiet. Thinking he needed to fill the silence, the young pastor started talking about this and that until, finally, he asked the Elder if he was going to say anything. After a long pause, the Elder said, "I asked you to come sit. I did not ask you to solve my problems or tell me about yours. Sometimes, your companionship is enough. If I need more, I will invite you into the conversation." The young pastor never forgot the lesson that sometimes people just need you to come alongside them and be there.

When someone is struggling, it can be helpful to give hope with facts. They may not realize that the symptoms they are experiencing are typical and help is available. Reassure them to help reduce their level of fear. Provide them with information – facts, next steps, and sources of additional support. A great way to start a conversation is, "I care about you, and I noticed a change in XYZ (whatever it is)." You don't need to go overboard with facts and resources – just be sure to share enough information that they can follow up with help if they need or want.

If the person needing help says they don't want help, don't push. Please encourage them to talk to someone they trust and never threaten them. Be patient and remain open and friendly as they may reach out for help in the future. Learn the resources in your area so if they need professional help, you can guide them in the right direction.

Remember, with our mental health, there are no set steps 1, 2, 3, or 4, and the ALGEE model was designed to be flexible, with you selecting the correct choice for the person and situation. Safety should always be the priority, and staying calm with a low voice can be helpful for anyone. Above all, you are not trying to "fix" the person; you want to give them hope by letting them know that what they are feeling doesn't last forever. They are not a burden.

We are all human, and no one is perfect. Lead with kindness, as we never know what someone else is going through. If you are the one struggling, reach out to someone you trust. There's a good chance that person wants to be a safe place for you to land during your challenges and to love you and support you along the way.

Everyone needs hope, but to move forward, we must be honest. Hope means believing that we can get where we want to go. Hope needs to know where we are headed and what our goals are. Lastly, hope needs to understand how we are going to get there. We can be hopeful, but without being honest about our starting point, our body knows we are lying to ourselves. Our body and mind need to believe what we are saying is true before we can move forward. Once we have worked on this, we can begin to make progress and help others along the way.

Thought to Carry with You

"Love recognizes no barriers. It jumps hurdles, leaps fences, penetrates walls to arrive at its destination full of hope." – Maya Angelou, from *The Complete Collected Poems of Maya Angelou*

JOURNAL PROMPTS

1. Do you have unprocessed trauma in your life? If so, have you journaled about it before? Have you talked to someone you trust about it? It's okay if you are not ready to unpack it yet. Just like our daughter, you need to be ready to unpack it; however, being aware of the trauma can be a start. Addressing the trauma when you are younger can help you put more tools in your toolbox of life to use with your family or others.

_____

_____

_____

_____

_____

_____

_____

_____

_____

_____

_____

_____

_____

_____

_____

2. How have you been feeling lately? Are there any red flags when you answer that question honestly? Have you been taking care of your body? Are you sleeping and eating right? Do you move every day?

_____

_____

_____

_____

_____

_____

_____

_____

_____

_____

_____

_____

_____

_____

_____

_____

3. I once wrote in my journal, " I can change my life story by putting a period at the end of the bad stuff with history and deciding what's next. I have spent energy blaming and hurting. I need to own the story and move on." I then poured my heart out writing about some difficult subjects. If you have anything lingering in the past that you want to deal with, I encourage you to try getting it out of your head and onto paper. You will see it differently, and it will lift a weight off your shoulders that you didn't even know you were carrying.

_____

_____

_____

_____

_____

_____

_____

_____

_____

_____

_____

_____

_____

_____

Resources

- Mental Health First Aid Training information can be found at https://www.mentalhealthfirstaid.org/

- Indigenous wellness article also found in the references:

  Demientieff, L.X., Frank, P. (2022). *I Remember Who I Am: Deg Xit'an Athabascan Perspectives on Wellness. In: Danto, D., Zangeneh, M. (eds) Indigenous Knowledge and Mental Health.* Springer, Cham. https://doi.org/10.1007/978-3-030-71346-1_13

- Books you can read that are helpful in unpacking our past:

  Own Your Past Change Your Future by Dr. John Delony

  Atlas of the Heart by Dr. Brené Brown

Chapter 8

THE CHAD STORY

There are moments in our lives that we never forget. Some moments are entwined with happiness, such as the birth of a child or the shared feeling when we watch an Olympic athlete overcome obstacles and win a gold medal. Other memories are tied to pain, like where we were when the 9/11 terrorist attacks occurred. Some memories are more personal, not on a national event level, but are etched in your mind forever. I remember exactly where I stood in the University of Alaska Fairbanks (UAF) hockey rink, watching my son practice with his team, when my daughter's phone call came through on March 9, 2020. All I heard was crying, which can only be described as deep, heart-wrenching sobs. My heart was squeezing with fear as I was telling her to take a breath. There was a pause before she said, "Mom, Chad's gone!" and then more sobs, no air. The world changed for many people that day; they would have to figure out how to continue without him.

I had met Chad Staley a few years earlier through our now son-in-law. They were teammates on the local college hockey team. Chad was one of the "brothers" we saw fairly regularly and became like family to our daughter. Chad had an infectious personality and was a natural leader on and off the ice. If Chad was in the room, you could be fairly certain that there would be laughter – lots of laughter and a good story to go with it. Although not large in stature, he was "big" in presence and how he made others feel. Amid the craziness, Chad would occasionally pause and say or share something profound or how much he loved and appreciated you. His family and friends clung to those memories after his passing.

During the spring of 2019, we had a few college students over for a home-cooked meal. One of those students was Chad. Chad and I sat at the table after supper, discussing his future career goals and planning after college. During the conversation, I must have commented on the immense work stress, the busyness of life and family, and how I had other dreams for life. He paused, looked me in the eye, and asked, "Why don't you just do it?" He explained his mom was making changes in her life and thought it was going to be a good thing for her. Our conversation continued, but his simple question would go on to plague my thoughts, creeping in as I found myself thinking more about it. I had even started looking for tools and ways to pursue something new. His uncanny ability to read people and to shift conversations, getting right to the heart of the matter, was an unusual gift.

Chad and I also talked about hockey. We were trying to figure out how to support our young son's love of hockey. I smiled as I watched Chad's face light up. He talked animatedly with his hands, telling different stories about his youth and junior hockey years. One of the things that became clear in the conversation was that Chad had made a lot of friends through hockey. He had a network of adventures and brothers throughout the United States, Canada, and other places in the hockey world. Since Chad was on the smaller size for a hockey player, he talked about learning to work twice as hard and not give up when it felt like he was being overlooked. He used those emotions as fuel to do more. He knew the world of sports and could talk about players and teams in just about any sport, but he loved hockey, and everyone knew his favorite hockey team was the Detroit Red Wings.

Chad played different sports as a child, but he fell in love with hockey and chose to pursue it beyond a recreational level. He grew up playing hockey in Washington state for the Tri-Cities Jr. Americans and Wenatchee Wild. He left his Kennewick, Washington, home to play junior hockey for the Spruce Kings in Prince George, Canada. He was eventually recruited from there to play college hockey for the University of Alaska Fairbanks (UAF), where he was reunited with some former teammates from youth and junior hockey. After graduating from UAF in the spring of 2019, he eventually found his way to play hockey in Europe in the fall of 2019.

Kids loved Chad. When he came to our house, it was not uncommon for him to challenge our son to an intense floor hockey game. Laughter and yelling could be heard from the basement as words of encouragement and challenges were spoken. Wherever he played hockey, he found a following, including handicapped and kids with special challenges. He had a soft heart for the less fortunate and was willing to help anyone. He was known for being a hard worker on the ice and a friend to everyone. He kept in regular contact with many of his friends and left a trail of adventures and "Chad" stories to be shared by close friends and acquaintances. I believe Chad saw every change of team as an opportunity for new adventures and new friends.

One of the habits Chad developed was texting or calling his friends when something reminded him of them, or he was doing something he thought they should be sharing. A friend described Chad as like the "energizer bunny" that would be buzzing around all over the place nonstop; yet, he would stop for the beautiful parts of life, like sunsets, and reach out to friends to share it with them. He made people feel special. He loved dogs. It was not unusual for him to befriend a dog wherever he was playing hockey, so there were dog stories to accompany his hockey stories.

In March 2020, Chad had just returned home from Europe after playing his first season of professional hockey in Germany and Italy. COVID-19 was closing things down in Europe, so he was glad to be home. Friends convinced him to participate in a local men's league hockey tournament, where Chad took a puck to the face, damaging some teeth. It would be a few days before he could get into the dentist, so he used a face shield and returned to the rink. However, the pain was pretty intense. A friend, trying to be helpful, gave Chad a little blue pill that they thought was prescription pain medication. Unfortunately, only a few hours later, when Chad's Mom went to get him for dinner, she only found his lifeless body. The little blue pill had been laced with fentanyl, killing him within minutes of taking it.

According to the Centers for Disease Control and Prevention, "Fentanyl is a synthetic opioid that is up to 50 times stronger than heroin and 100 times stronger than morphine."[1] Prescription opioids flooded the market in the 1990s and 2000s as an option for treating severe pain. Fentanyl was developed in a lab as an alternative to a plant-based opioid because of the need. The National Institute of Health (NIH) explains that more than 50 million adults in the United States live with chronic pain.[2] Synthetic opioids, like fentanyl, are now the leading cause of overdose deaths since 2016.[3] Only a tiny bit of fentanyl, 2 milligrams, can kill someone. Other drugs laced with fentanyl are killing unexpected people.[4]

Although some fentanyl is tied to addiction, the majority of cases are accidental deaths like Chad's. Family and friends worried at first about sharing how he died, thinking people who did not know him would think he had a drug problem, which was not the case. Chad had so much to live for and was happy, thinking about new possibilities. My last message back and forth with him was about the hockey camp he was starting to plan. I had been hoping my son would be able to participate. Chad's life, unfortunately, serves as an example that one should not take drugs not prescribed to you, and you should know the source.

Chad made an impact wherever he played hockey, but it seemed especially huge in Prince George, where the Chad Staley Memorial Athletic Foundation was created to help develop skills and opportunities for less fortunate kids to play sports. Prince George is also home to the Chad Staley Memorial Arena. The UAF Nanooks Men's Hockey Team also presents the Chad Staley Team Player of the Year Award every year in memory of Chad.

Chad Staley was an incredible human being who was doing good things. He was a friend to everyone. He was a great person who made a bad decision, not knowing it would be his last. As his mom, Jennifer Staley, shared at a postponed memorial gathering in the spring of 2022, "It was one hit, one pill, and game over forever."

Grief can hit hard as it involves our emotions, intellect, spirit, and physical parts of us. The process we walk through is not linear but rather full of ups and downs, twists and turns. Losing someone like Chad, who had friends and family scattered over thousands of miles, can be challenging in the best of scenarios. COVID-19 complicated the grief as people were not allowed to gather and grieve collectively as they had in the past. The National Library of Medicine published an article by Arora and Bhatia that explained that grief during COVID-19 was missing the normal social support, mourning rituals, and the general mourning process.[5] These factors can lead to complicated grief that can cause prolonged grief disorder. Some of the techniques the authors suggested to process grief was directed journaling and retelling the narrative of the death. Both mentioned techniques help one process the loss.

When we talk about grief, one conversation that can get lost is grief that involves children. Chad was loved and a fan favorite for any of the children he spent time with as a player. Grief looks different for the developmental stages of a child. For example, our son was almost twelve at the time of Chad's passing, so he understood that death meant he wasn't going to see Chad in person again. At that age, children want to understand what happened and are concerned about how things will change moving forward. They also tend to identify strongly with the person who passes away. I didn't know that normal reactive behavior included being upset that things had changed and looking for someone to blame. There can be an increase in anxiety and denial, as well as trouble concentrating and sleeping. Parents need to keep in mind that these behaviors may not show up right away, so it is easy to think they are general behavioral issues rather than grief manifesting itself several months later.

Adults and children need a healthy outlet and permission to express their feelings through art, writing, and other activities like exercise. Children need their questions answered, their feelings validated, love and reassurance, and to be heard. Without recognizing the cause, it can be easy for the wrong conversations to take place, leading the child and adult down a frustrating path and some unhealthy behaviors.

If you or someone you love has lost someone special and you are noticing behavioral changes, pause and be curious. Why are they acting that way? Why am I choosing to do something I know is wrong? It can be powerful to stop and ask the question Dr. Bruce Perry and Oprah Winfrey used as a title for their book, *What Happened to You?*, versus asking the judgmental question, "What's wrong with you?"[6]

Children simply do not have the processing capabilities that adults do. Their brains are not fully developed with the connections for working the part of the brain that helps them understand the varying aspects of death. If adults do not help the child with the processing, this trauma stays with them and can create more significant challenges as they move through their teens and into adult life.

If you or your loved one are struggling with grief, please know that sometimes we need to add new tools to our life skills toolbox. During one stretch of extreme grief, I reached out to a counselor to help me make sense of what was happening and to help me put a plan together for myself and our son. Things did not go perfectly, but I had a plan I could use that had been thought out ahead of time while I was calm and in a good headspace.

When we lose someone suddenly and unexpectedly, like Chad, it is important to process the loss. It can be important for people who loved the person to feel that their death made a positive impact, so they seek ways to use it to benefit others. Information about the death may be shared to help inform others and educate the public. The death may be used to create a call of action when combined with others going through a similar experience. Chad's parents showed great courage in being willing to talk about his death and make others aware. Their courage allowed me to have important conversations with my son as he entered his teen years.

Let's share a little bit of kindness and do our part to help ensure other families and friends do not experience a tragedy like this. Be a friend, support the less fortunate, and keep a little bit of Chad in your heart.

Thought to Carry with You

"You find that you have peace of mind and you can enjoy yourself, get more sleep, and rest when you know that it was one hundred percent effort that you gave – win or lose." – Gordie Howe, *And... Howe! An Authorized Autobiography*. Gordie Howe was a legendary hockey player and Chad's favorite player.

JOURNAL PROMPTS

1. Have you lost anyone close to you due to a tragedy? Were you able to process their passing? Have you journaled about their passing? If not, maybe think about the time surrounding their passing and the events that followed. As you read through what you wrote, can you identify any emotions that feel unprocessed? Don't be afraid to reach out for help in processing those emotions.

_____

_____

_____

_____

_____

_____

_____

_____

_____

_____

_____

_____

_____

2. Try writing a letter to the person you lost unexpectedly. Say all the things you wish you could have said to them.

_____

_____

_____

_____

_____

_____

_____

_____

_____

_____

_____

_____

_____

_____

_____

_____

_____

_____

_____

3. Consider what you could do to help make the passing help others. Is there an organization to which you could donate your time or money? Was there any cause important to the person to which you might help bring awareness? What action could you take in memory of the individual you lost?

_____

_____

_____

_____

_____

_____

_____

_____

_____

_____

_____

_____

_____

_____

_____

_____

_____

_____

_____

_____

Resources

After reading this, perhaps you have realized that you or someone you love could also use some help. Below, you find a list of places that can direct you in the right direction.

Crisis? Please call or text 988 to talk to someone

- SAMHSA (Substance Abuse and Mental Health Services Administration) is a general informational resource.

  https://www.samhsa.gov/find-help/national-helpline

  or 1-800-662-4357

- The National Institute of Health has the HEAL project, where you can find information on the Opioid Crisis: https://heal.nih.gov/

- A great place for dealing with grief, especially with children, is https://good-grief.org/resources/

- An overall resource that focuses on help for when you are grieving and advice on how to help others that are grieving is https://optionb.org/

Chapter 9

THE ADDICTION

S
ometimes, pain sneaks up on us. We thought we were having innocent fun or even participating in something good for us. Eventually, something seems off when you realize you "need" that experience, drink, or drug again. My parents did a good job of instilling the fear of what would happen if I got involved with things I shouldn't. Being seven years younger than my brother, I can remember holding fence posts for him to pound into the ground with a sledgehammer for several hours after he had arrived home in the early morning hours after a night of partying with his friends. My dad never said a word, but he sure made us work hard that day. I remember watching my brother wince as the sledgehammer made contact with the post. Despite learning about potential consequences and, for the most part, avoiding anything that could land me in fence-post fixing duty, I began a journey that would give me empathy for those struggling with addictions.

It all began innocently enough. I attended high school in the mid-1980s when popular actresses were paper thin, like Molly Ringwald in the movie *The Breakfast Club*. All the girls were starving themselves, desperate to fit into popular culture. Girls would quietly talk about how you could make yourself throw up after you ate a meal and all the latest diet fads. One day at lunch, one of the girls shared how proud they were of their mother. She had lost forty pounds and looked great. The girl joked she was worried she would end up with another little sibling to watch because her mom looked so great her dad couldn't keep his hands off her. After the laughter died down, everyone wanted to know how she had lost the weight. The girl explained that when her mom felt hungry, she would drink diet soda instead of eating. I remember thinking I didn't like gagging myself to vomit, but I could drink diet soda. Thus began my journey with my diet soda addiction.

Even though I considered my extra 10-15 pounds a problem, I never once thought of my diet soda as a problem. I can remember being generous in college by sharing my groceries with roommates as long as you didn't touch my diet soda, hard pretzels, and cheese to go with the pretzels. I considered them study staples for getting through the long hours of homework and assignments. I continued that thought process as I worked through graduate school and into my first full-time job. It wasn't until my first pregnancy that I questioned the impact of diet soda on my body.

At the time of my first pregnancy, the literature was pretty clear that if we cared about our baby, we would consider that the baby was eating what we were eating. If we wanted a healthy baby, we needed to eat healthy. When I realized I needed to cut back or stop drinking diet soda, I wasn't thinking about all the chemicals. I was focused on caffeine and how my baby might not grow properly and be born addicted to caffeine. The pregnancy made me realize how often I reached for a diet soda. I had it as a beverage of choice at my meals and during the day to pick me up when I was tired. A mother's love is strong, and I remember it getting easier after the first few weeks because I was determined not to hurt my baby.

I returned to my old habits after I weaned our first child from breastfeeding only a few months after she was born. I noticed it was harder to wean myself entirely with the second pregnancy. I remember having a conversation with my doctor because I felt guilty that I had given in and was having one occasionally. The doctor started to laugh and explain there were far worse things, and if I was keeping it to one a day, the baby would not be affected. I wasn't sure I agreed, but I found myself having half of a can or bottle of soda once or twice a week during stressful stretches of the pregnancy. I felt guilty because of the chemicals, but the relief seemed worth the trade-off. I would go for stretches of weeks without it, but if life got stressful, I would have a few sips or a small glass of it.

When we moved several hours away from a grocery store and town, I could not deny I might have an addiction. One of our neighbors who lived a few miles up the road by dog team or snow machine in the winter would stop by on her way to check the mail in the nearby village. She would ask if I needed anything, and I would ask her if she could get me a diet soda. There were a few shelves of mostly outdated groceries in the same area as the post office, and they tended to keep a few sodas in stock. I can remember being devastated when the neighbor would return without a diet soda because they didn't have any. Life was too hectic at that time for me to stop and spend too much time on the challenge of quitting, but it was starting to be on my radar.

A few years later, after working desk jobs while also helping to keep our small business afloat, I could no longer deny I had an issue when a coworker casually handed me a printout of an article that warned about the dangers of diet soda. I had no idea soda could be used as a degreaser and for cleaning rusty parts. The article made me pause and start to think about it differently, but dang, it tasted good. By then, I had switched brands because I had been told that one had more caffeine, and I was drinking it to help me stay awake. I rationalized that there were way worse things to put into my body. It was what I wanted when I was stressed, and diet soda became my drink of choice all day long. I do remember at one point attending a women's study group at church where we were focusing on weight loss, and I realized other women struggled with a soda addiction. One friend even mentioned that she had looked into how smokers dealt with quitting to try to figure out how she could quit. At least I knew I wasn't alone. I started paying more attention and attempted to cut back, but I never really stopped as long as I was working or life was stressful.

We moved to town in 2009 so that my husband could attend college and for me to find work while still trying to raise kids and keep our other home two hours away maintained. Days were long and nights short, but I was teaching at the local university, and I loved it. My diet soda intake increased, as did my struggle to lose weight. My husband and I made progress in weight loss in 2012 when we devoted ourselves to a stringent Keto diet, which also meant giving up my diet soda. I did fairly well, but after several weeks, I found myself having one occasionally. Once again, as the stress increased, so did my desire to have a diet soda. I knew my habit had become a part of my identity when coworkers would show up with a diet soda for me when I was especially busy or stressed. I even got a 12-pack for my birthday one year.

One of my former department chairs had me come to her office to discuss an issue. As the meeting wrapped up, she mentioned seeing me frequently with a can of diet soda. I explained that I had never really gotten into drinking coffee and turned to this instead. She paused, leaned back into her chair, and asked if I remembered that she had a work life prior to academia. I nodded my head quietly in agreement. She shared how she used to drink soda like water, but that changed after one of her former welding jobs. The job took place at a large soda manufacturing plant where almost everything they worked on involved high-level hazmat training. She said she looked around the plant one day and realized all those toxic chemicals they were working around were being used to create the can of soda I held in my hand. How could that possibly be good for us? I shook my head and said I would keep it in mind.

When packing for fishing or hunting adventures, I would make sure I had all the essentials needed for camp, including my diet soda. I would calculate how many days we would be away and try to ensure I had enough – with one emergency stash in my bag. I remember thinking to myself, "I am like a person struggling with alcohol and keeping a private stash, so I am sure I can have one." I would get anxious if I miscalculated, and it looked like I might run out before returning. I would portion out the last one, trying to make it last.

I continued to drink it as my beverage of choice, especially when life got stressful. I would work on tapering off or even quitting for a while, but sure enough, life would get stressful, and I would eventually start again. After losing my mom to cancer in

2018, my body was giving signals that I needed to give it some attention. At one point, I was so sick I couldn't drive myself to the doctor. I suffered from a parasite that was robbing my body of nutrients and energy. I struggled to get through my days and would start my day with a diet soda to help me wake up and continue drinking it throughout the day, trying to stay awake and function. I realized I was averaging 4-8 diet sodas a day!

By the fall of 2018, I was desperate and found myself at the doctor's office once again asking for help. I was told my thyroid was not functioning and that with sleep and watching my diet, my weight would start to regulate again. I wasn't making much progress. By the spring of 2019, I needed something different. I reached out to a health coach who practiced in functional medicine. I had finally found someone who listened and acknowledged my struggles. She was willing to try to help me as I made some significant lifestyle changes after realizing my adrenals were shot, and without them, my whole body's system was off.

So, what is the big deal with drinking diet soda? Nothing, if you can just have one occasionally and not think about making sure you can have another one when you "need" it. My addiction to diet soda involved both aspects of addiction – both chemical and behavioral. Looking back, I kept a folder of articles and clippings on diet soda and, at one point, thought I would start a group on Facebook for addicts of diet soda. I was embarrassed and never really pushed it out there, but I thought that if I struggled, maybe someone else was too. I lost track of how many people would tell me there are worse things to be addicted to, and although I believed them, it does not negate that it is an addiction.

The earliest article I kept was a 2001 email that discussed the importance of water and the uses of soda for cleaning. The email claimed that troopers used soda to clean blood off the highway, and you could use it for cleaning toilet bowls, removing rust spots, cleaning corrosion around battery terminals, and removing grease from clothes. The author, a pharmacist, was trying to encourage the reader to drink water rather than soda, but it seemed extreme. After a few internet searches, I discovered these statements made for some excellent home science experiments and YouTube videos. Because the active ingredient in soda is phosphoric acid with a pH of 2.8, it can be used to clean some minor rust spots and remove tarnish from coins; however, it would take a lot longer than four days for a nail to dissolve in the soda and troopers have the blood removed with other more powerful cleaners meant to deal with biological fluids.

What was interesting in my research was the effort companies made to make sure that we knew that the acidic level of certain citrus fruits is the same or lower than the pH of the soda. Specifically, lemon, lime juice, and vinegar have a lower pH than soda.[1] Whether the website or article mentioned that you were comparing the pH of a naturally growing fruit versus a drink made up of a mix of naturally occurring and manufactured chemicals varied with the authorship of the websites or articles.

Another article I saved was a July 2012 MSNBC.msn.com (now Today.com) post by Emily Main that gave five reasons to kick your soda habit. The five reasons were:

"1) Accelerated aging due to phosphates and phosphoric acid in the soda; too much phosphate and phosphoric acid in our body can lead to heart and kidney problems, muscle loss, and osteoporosis.

"2) Caramel cancer-causers used in the production to create the coloring of the brown-colored sodas.

"3) 'Mountain Dew Mind' – a condition due to the brominated vegetable oil (BVO) added, the same chemical used as a flame retardant in plastics.

4) Toxic cans – aluminum cans are lined with bisphenol-A (BPA) which is an epoxy resin known to interfere with hormones and cause cancer.

"5) Water pollution – due to the artificial sweeteners used in diet sodas that enter the waterways, the sweeteners pass right through our bodies without breaking down into something else."[2]

It was interesting to discover that after studies were done citing concerns over the chemicals, the soda companies reformulated their caramel coloring to lower the 4-methylimidazole, which is known to cause cancer but deemed safe at certain amounts. Despite the changes, according to a Consumer Reports study, there appear to be variations in the amount found in products.[3] Many manufacturers have also changed their formulations to remove the BVO, which is used not only in soda but also in popular sports drinks. Although still technically allowed in the United States, it was banned in the European Union, Japan, and other countries. However, as of November 2, 2023, the United States Food and Drug Administration (FDA) proposed to revoke the use of BVO.[4]

Interestingly, for me and all of my challenges, one of the main findings of several studies was the impact BVO had on the thyroid. "Results from these studies demonstrate bioaccumulation of bromine and toxic effects on the thyroid – a gland that produces hormones that play a key role in regulating blood pressure, body temperature, heart rate, metabolism and the reaction of the body to other hormones."[5]

In researching the concern of BPA, I learned it was the chemical used in polycarbonate (clear) plastics and epoxy resins. I knew about BPA and plastics because articles started appearing around 2008, when our son was born, warning us to use BPA-free baby bottles, sippy cups, and water bottles due to the impact on infants and children. What I didn't realize was that BPA, in its epoxy resin form, is used inside many soda cans to keep the acids in the soda from reacting with the metal. According to a Mayo Clinic article, "Some research has shown that BPA can seep into food or beverages from containers made with BPA. Exposure to BPA is a concern because of the possible health effects on the brain and prostate gland of fetuses, infants, and children. It can also affect children's behavior. Additional research suggests a possible link between BPA and increased blood pressure, type 2 diabetes and cardiovascular disease."[6] The FDA has cited several studies that indicate that low levels of BPA are safe, so they will continue to monitor rather than ban it at this point.

The topic of artificial sweeteners was one that I felt I understood as it was one of the most cited reasons that I was aware of for quitting. I had heard and read how artificial sweeteners could trigger the desire for more sugar and possibly alter the brain to need and desire more. I felt my addiction fell in line with this reasoning. However, I had never considered the impact on our water supply and the possible impacts on the organisms, fish, and wildlife.

Although some of the concerns in the 2001 email were debunked as myths, it is disturbing to realize that some are not, and those that were debunked are more like exaggerations rather than complete untruths. The second article helped educate consumers on issues that needed to be addressed. A quick internet search will reveal a list of health concerns surrounding diet soda. Most of the health concerns mentioned are centered around artificial sweeteners, weight struggles, acidity impact on your teeth and bone density, caffeine content, metabolic syndrome, diabetes, negative effects on gut health, and possible negative impacts on the kidney.

My struggle is real. If my head knows all those facts, why do I still struggle? Why is it so hard to quit? Diet soda combines artificial sweeteners and caffeine from a chemical equation. The sweeteners release dopamine in our brain, which is tied to our pleasure and reward system, keeping us in a loop of cravings.[7] Caffeine is a stimulant that can create physical dependence. If consumed enough, you can begin to build a tolerance that means you need to increase the amount you consume to get the same effect.[8] Caffeine levels would explain why when I would try to stop drinking diet soda suddenly, I would suffer from constant headaches, feel on edge with everyone, and feel tired. My addiction also involved a behavioral addiction in that I had created a habit of drinking it. It was associated with my mornings, driving, working at my desk, and other activities where I would find myself opening a can before I even thought about it. I also tied it to emotional factors by reaching for it and desiring it whenever I was experiencing stress or fatigue.

The pain caused by my years of consumption of diet soda had caught up with me. My thyroid and adrenals were no longer functioning properly. I felt a constant brain fog and fatigue. I do not have a story of street drugs or alcohol addiction, but I would challenge you to consider how you define addiction. Time Magazine did a special edition on addiction and pointed out that our addictions have changed over time as an American society. Our addiction battles now include alcohol, drugs, tobacco, caffeine, food, gambling, shopping, sex, and the internet.[9]

In realizing my challenges, my empathy for others struggling with addictions grew. Michael D. Lemonick, in his article on *The Science of Addiction,* defined addiction as "a chronic relapsing of behavior in the face of negative consequences; the overwhelming urge to continue something you know is bad for you."[10] Addictions are generally grouped into substance addiction or behavioral addiction. The causes and risk factors vary but typically consider genetics, environmental, and psychological. We will often point to physical, behavioral, or psychological signs when trying to define an addiction. The addiction will eventually impact the person's life in all areas, whether it be their health, relationships, or societal interaction.

If we recognize an addiction, whether a substance-based or behavioral-based one, what do we do? I wish I had a magic formula that would fix everything. Since addictions tend to grow over time and involve our bodies, habits, environments, etc., the healing process is also individualized. I do not mean that the journey is on your own, but rather that the treatment and recovery will be individualized according to what works for your body and lifestyle. If you don't know where to start your journey, ask for help. Your regular physician can be a great starting point, or many employers offer programs where you can work with an independent agency to help you locate appropriate services.

You can also search for licensed therapists through www.psychologytoday.com. Your detoxification may involve deciding whether you are done and dealing with the physical withdrawals on your own, or it may mean checking into a facility that offers a detoxification program or process. New medications are emerging to help in the recovery processes of alcohol, tobacco, and certain other drug addictions. Several therapies that are now more widely available have been helping people find relief, such as Cognitive Behavior Therapy (CBT), Dialectical Behavior Therapy (DBT), and Eye-Movement Desensitization and Reprocessing (EMDR). Another essential part of the journey for many people includes some community with accountability, generally found in support groups around the addiction area. Some of the more well-known support groups are Alcoholics Anonymous (AA), Narcotics Anonymous (NA), SMART Recovery, and Celebrate Recovery.

When looking at our journey to wellness, it can also be helpful to remember to take a holistic approach to the process. I attended a Traditional Path for Indigenous Wellness through Peer Support training by Muskeg Wellness, where we discussed the importance of traditional diets in the role of healing. While walking through the treatment and recovery steps mentioned above, many people find healing in the foods they eat. Whole, natural foods tied to our ancestors' land can help heal our gut, which often helps heal the brain.[11] The trainers also challenged us to develop our definition of recovery. I defined recovery as the ongoing ability to stay connected with family (however you define that for yourself), community, and culture. Ongoing and connection are the key concepts for me. We are all a work in process, and if we have dealt with an addiction, we know we have to continue to make choices in the right direction. Although we hope it gets easier, we are still making choices. Making good choices can be easier if we choose connections through a community and our culture.

If you have walked through the pain of addiction, consider how you can use that pain for growth. How can I grow from what I went through? What can I learn? How might I be able to use it to help others? Perhaps you can use your pain to comfort others or, at the very least, give them hope.

Thought to Carry with You

"When you replace judgment with curiosity, everything changes." – Robyn Conley Downs, author of *The Feel-Good Effect: Reclaim Your Wellness by Creating Small Shifts That Create Big Change*

JOURNAL PROMPTS

1. Do you struggle with an addiction? It does not have to be drugs or alcohol. It can be a behavior like gambling or always scrolling on our phones. Have you talked to someone about it? Have you journaled about your addiction? Are you taking care of yourself – eating, sleeping, and exercising (even just walking)? Have you considered reaching out for professional help?

_____

_____

_____

_____

_____

_____

_____

_____

_____

_____

_____

_____

_____

_____

_____

_____

2. Do you have someone who can support you in this journey of change? Is there someone that can help you stay accountable or help you find resources you might need? Having someone to talk to who is not "judging" you but walking alongside you is valuable. What would you find helpful during your journey of change?

_____

_____

_____

_____

_____

_____

_____

_____

_____

_____

_____

_____

_____

_____

_____

_____

_____

_____

3. We have a basic need for connection, and when we struggle with an addiction, it has been shown that support groups can be helpful, especially ones that have experienced something similar. Are you open to trying something like that? Consider why you are or are not open to it? Is there a way for you to find additional support?

_____

_____

_____

_____

_____

_____

_____

_____

_____

_____

_____

_____

_____

_____

_____

_____

_____

Resources

If you feel someone in your life could use some help, please don't be afraid to reach out.

Crisis? Please call or text 988 to talk to someone; you can also access help through 988lifeline.org

- A general informational resource is SAMHSA (Substance Abuse and Mental Health Services Administration. https://www.samhsa.gov/find-help/national-helpline   or 1-800-662-4357

- NAMI (National Alliance on Mental Illness) Helpline is 1-800-950-6264. You can also find resources and support at https://www.nami.org/

- Information on HALT, a helpful technique for identifying triggers that lead to addictive behaviors: https://bradford-health.com/halt-hunger-anger-loneliness-tiredness/

Chapter 10

THE RIDE

When I finished my undergraduate degree in 1990, my parents gave me a trip to the West Coast of the United States to visit family. It was my first adventure all by myself. One stop was visiting my uncle and aunt in California. My uncle was much older than my dad and served his country honorably as a pilot in World War II, the Korean War, and the Vietnam War. In World War II, he was taken prisoner of war in Germany after his plane had been shot down. As he aged, his body continued to bear the burden of his service to his country, enduring physical challenges from his time in combat. I listened to the stories they shared and treasured my time with them. I appreciated my aunt, making sure I saw different parts of their community, from the beaches to a rodeo and the local college.

When it came time to leave, I was planning to take the bus from their town to a community a few hours north to visit my cousin. I made it to the bus station. I was feeling a little overwhelmed, having never used the bus system before. A miscommunication at the bus station meant I missed the bus. I used the payphone to call my aunt, unsure what to do. I am sure I must have had a bit of panic in my voice. A few minutes later, my elderly aunt showed up in her large sedan car and yelled, "Get in!"

My aunt moved that car along at a good clip, and we made it to the next bus stop ahead of the bus I was supposed to be on. I was able to board the bus at the next station and finish the rest of my trip. On the way, I must have said thank you a hundred times, feeling stupid and silly for missing the bus. I asked her what I owed her, as I knew she had not only given me her time driving the crazy throughways but also spent gas at California prices. I remember her telling me, "You owe me a pay-it-forward. I must have given a quizzical look as she continued, "At some point in the future, someone will need your help, and it may cost you something, whether it is time, money, or inconvenience. I ask you to pay it forward by helping that person – that will be enough payment for me." I took a deep breath, trying to take in her request. I promised I would and thanked her again. She had given me an action lesson on kindness.

I hope I have paid it forward more than once. The stories in this book are filled with people that were there for others. My family has been blessed with good-hearted people. I want that for my children, grandchildren, great-grandchildren, and beyond. We need a world that values connections and relationships – to be there for each other. COVID-19 changed how we connect, and I think we have only begun to see its impact, especially on our younger generation. We need to be open to dealing with our hurts and traumas so that we can heal and pass on the right things to future generations. Dealing with the past now can lead to better relationships, communication, and healing. So how can we get there?

A few years back, when something bad happened, I used to push down my emotions and avoid facing them. I would not have allowed myself to ride the wave of grief. I know I am in a better place now, having learned not to fight my feelings. I understand that growth comes from it. I know my body keeps score, and I need to pay attention to it. It is okay to remind myself that I will be okay and that it makes sense to feel this way. I know that I am not alone. I can have difficult conversations and get help if I need it. I am willing to do the work and change things if needed. I remind myself that I am changing the family tree by listening to the sirens from the past and dealing with them. One area in the field of epigenetics (the study of changes in organisms) examines how changes in the gene expression or cellular phenotype can be influenced by the environment and life experiences and passed down to future generations. This includes intergenerational trauma and how trauma can be passed down from one generation to the next. Your trauma and stress not only impacts you but potentially impacts your children. The good news is that identifying and healing your trauma responses can bring a more balanced state and a reversal of the damage, which can also be passed down.[1]

Learning to acknowledge and process our emotions are steps in addressing the trauma, whether the big trauma (natural disasters, tragic loss of a loved one) or a little trauma (events that cause constant overwhelm and stress). If left unchecked, trauma causes us to disconnect from the people around us and what our body is trying to tell us. When we delve into our past, we need to be aware that we can become more vulnerable and sensitive, possibly leading to reliance on drugs, alcohol, overeating, overspending, and avoidance to cope with our emotions.

Different techniques and coping strategies have been developed to help us as we unpack our past. A good first step, which can often be the most difficult, is pausing and naming what you feel – hurt, angry, critical, rejected, confused, helpless, insecure, embarrassed, etc. It might be helpful to initially use a list of feelings to help you name what you are experiencing. You can Google "list of feeling words," and several options will appear. It's not about finding a perfect list, just one that will help you identify and name your feelings. As you get better at this, you will get better at helping your child name their feelings when something is happening to them. I found a list, printed it, and taped it to the bathroom mirror to practice naming my feelings beyond sad, mad, and glad.

After you have named your feeling, pay attention to where in your body you feel it and what it feels like; for example, I might feel worry in my chest – tight and contracted. Is it feeling heavy, tingling, hot, cold, or radiating? You can then focus on relaxing your breathing. The circular breathing technique is to breathe in slowly for five seconds, hold your breath for five seconds, exhale slowly for five seconds, and repeat the process five times. Many people call it 5-5-5 breathing, so it is easy to remember.

As you listen to your body and breathe, reassure yourself that you are okay and it makes sense that you feel this way. Remember, you are loved. If you struggle with thinking of someone who loves you, remember God the Creator loves you. You should feel the intensity of the emotion start to subside. Then, try to identify the thought that caused the emotion to be activated and ask yourself if there is a different thought you can replace the original one with that won't act as a trigger.

Another technique you can use is to write your feelings down. Like I mentioned in chapter one, writing uses a part of your brain that is different from your emotions, so the simple act of writing can interrupt your thoughts enough to create a different pathway or new thought. While learning to identify and process your feelings, you can also engage in healthy hobbies or activities you enjoy. It can be something like joining a basketball league, gardening, running, beading, or crocheting; just make sure it is something you enjoy. Think about people you trust to encourage you as you walk through this healing journey and spend time with them.

If you struggle with sleep, another tool that can be helpful is a breathing exercise that can help redirect your thoughts by focusing on your breathing. The technique is called the Buteyko Short Inhale and Long Exhale. You inhale with a four-count and exhale for a count of six, repeating slowly and steadily.

In Dr. Alexandra Swenson-Ridley's book, *Unearthing Selfless Syndrome*, she explains the RELEASE method that she has successfully used with clients. As Swenson-Ridley describes it, the method has three pillars: shift, stabilize, sustain. When attempting to make healthy and healing changes, we must shift our thoughts from the subconscious to the conscious. When we stabilize, we are letting go of the past and being curious enough to create the new. Sustain involves the creation of the new and being willing to continue to let go, not because someone else wants it, but because you do.[2]

We must be willing to work hard to change the family tree. Our children deserve it. You deserve it. It is important to acknowledge that sometimes we need professional help. Often, the place to start is with your regular doctor, who can ensure you do not have other medical challenges and refer you to a mental health professional. I can only wish that the people around me had more skills and understanding when I was in the accident with my grandma and my hometown was destroyed by the tornado. We understand so much more about the brain and trauma now than when I was a child. I grew up in the "bootstraps" generation; when bad things happened, you picked yourself up, stuffed your emotions down, and worked harder.

We may find we need to have challenging conversations as we work on ourselves. According to author and pastor Craig Groeschel, there are three questions you should ask yourself before you communicate, whether that be sharing with an audience or having a difficult conversation with someone. Planning and thinking ahead can help you convey a clear message, which can be challenging to do with people we are close to. The first question to ask yourself is: "What do I want them to know?" Be clear about your intentions. The second question is: "What do I want them to feel?" This question highlights the importance of sharing facts but acknowledges that facts alone are not enough to inspire action. The third question is: "What do I want them to do?" You want to have one clear action or outcome the listener can do by naming it and giving direction on how they can do it. This clarity is vital for moving people forward from the why to the how.[3]

You can use these questions with family and friends. This framework of communication would have been helpful for me early in my marriage when I knew I needed to have difficult conversations but didn't know how to. I suspect I could have used it to convey my stress during the year of fear with the neighbors.

When dealing with difficult situations, it can be helpful to remember to slow our reactions, recognize that there might be something behind the behavior we are dealing with, and be intentional about our responses. It is essential that we remind ourselves and those we converse with that we care about them, they belong, and we have choices. I wish I would have had these skills when dealing with our children when we lost the baby, as well as when our daughter went through her challenges.

Ultimately, it comes down to healing. I hope in reading this book, you can imagine what it is like to wake up and know that even if you have painful memories that trigger you or new hurts happen, you are okay. You can journal, reach out to someone, and work through things enough to say sorry when needed and not engage in drama when prompted. You can live in a peaceful state rather than in chaos. You can add tools to your toolbox. You are changing your legacy. Maybe you will end up touching lives like Chad did.

In Demientieff and Frank's work on wellness, they shared several culturally-based suggestions and lessons related to wellness: "One lesson is that no human or community or culture is perfect and that ceremonies were created and used because life is challenging and can topple us out of balance. Together, and with love and compassion for each other, we can move through grief, find joy, and create our best lives on this earth."[4] I hope I left you with some practical thoughts on how to do that when dealing with addictions. We need each other.

My hope for you is that you are living your best life by being willing to do the hard work necessary to be at peace with your past. You are unique and the only you that will ever be, so make the most of it!

Thoughts to Carry with You

"Our feelings constitute a wonderful 'warning system' that tells us when we need to focus on a certain danger area in our lives or something that needs our love and attention. But when we are in denial, we bury these feelings – we push them into our unconscious like pushing giant beach balls under water. When a ball does get loose, it comes up with exaggerated force at an angle and may hurt someone – like a beach ball that has been pushed far under water and finally pops to the surface." – Keith Miller from his book, *The Taste of New Wine*.

"Only when we have the courage to own our history are we able to write a brave new ending to our story." - Brené Brown from her book *Rising Strong*

JOURNAL PROMPTS

1. Have you seen progress as you have tried journaling? Do you feel like you have made progress on your healing? Have you named any emotions and used a technique as you listened to your body?

---

2. What techniques and activities are you open to trying to help address your emotions?

_____

_____

_____

_____

_____

_____

_____

_____

_____

_____

_____

_____

_____

_____

_____

_____

_____

_____

_____

3. Have you identified any reactions that you have that are due to events from your childhood? If so, what are they? Have you thought about how you can teach your child skills they could use now to deal with their emotions? Think through and list some activities you could do with your children.

_____

_____

_____

_____

_____

_____

_____

_____

_____

_____

_____

_____

_____

_____

_____

_____

_____

_____

_____

_____

Resources

As mentioned at the beginning of the book, each chapter could be expanded into its own book by exploring the complex topics that are intertwined when dealing with life. I have added some more readings that you can explore if you want to dive into these topics further.

Crisis? Please call or text 988 to talk to someone; you can also access help through 988lifeline.org

- A general informational resource is SAMHSA (Substance Abuse and Mental Health Services Administration:. https://www.samhsa.gov/find-help/national-helpline or 1-800-662-4357

- Demientieff, L.X., Frank, P. (2022). *I Remember Who I Am: Deg Xit'an Athabascan Perspectives on Wellness. In: Danto, D., Zangeneh, M. (eds) Indigenous Knowledge and Mental Health.* Springer, Cham. https://doi.org/10.1007/978-3-030-71346-1_13

- Books

  The Body Keeps the Score: Brain, Mind, and Body in the Healing of Trauma by Bessel van der Kolk

  Winning the War of your Mind: Change Your Thinking, Change Your Life by Craig Groeschel

NOTES

Chapter 1: The Why

1. Winfrey, Oprah, and Bruce D. Perry. 2021. *What Happened to You? Conversations on Trauma, Resilience, and Healing.* N.p.: Flatiron Books. 100-104

2. NeuroRelay. 2013. "How Does Writing Affect Your Brain?" NeuroRelay. http://neurorelay.com/2013/08/07/how-does-writing-affect-your-brain/.

3. James, Karin H., and Laura Engelhardt. 2012. "The effects of handwriting experience on functional brain development in pre-literate children." *Trends in Neuroscience and Education* 1, no. 1 (December): 32-42. https://doi.org/10.1016/j.tine.2012.08.001.

4. Van der Weel, F. R., and Audrey L. Van der Meer. 2024. "Handwriting but not typewriting leads to widespread brain connectivity: a high-density EEG study with implications for the classroom." *Frontiers in Psychology* 14, no. 2023 (January). 10.3389/fpsyg.2023.1219945.

5. Smyth, J. M., A. A. Stone, A. Hurewitz, and A. Kaell. 1999. "Effects of Writing About Stressful Experiences on

Symptom Reduction in Patients With Asthma or Rheumatoid Arthritis: A Randomized Trial." *JAMA* 281, no. 14 (April): 1304-1309. doi:10.1001/jama.281.14.1304.

6. Van der Kolk, Bessel A. 2015. *The Body Keeps the Score: Brain, Mind, and Body in the Healing of Trauma.* New York, New York: Penguin Publishing Group. 26-27

Chapter 2: The Accident

1. US Department of Transportation National Highway Traffic Safety Administration. 2023. "Drunk Driving | Statistics and Resources." NHTSA. https://www.nhtsa. gov/risky-driving/drunk-driving.

2. Schaefer, Carol. 2006. *Grandmothers Counsel the World: Women Elders Offer Their Vision for Our Planet.* N.p.: Shambhala.

3. US Department of Transportation National Highway Traffic Safety Administration. 2023. "Drunk Driving | Statistics and Resources." NHTSA. https://www.nhtsa. gov/risky-driving/drunk-driving.

Chapter 3: The Window

1. Sleptzoff, Nick. 1985. "Weather.gov > State College, PA > May 31, 1985 Tornado Outbreak: 35th Anniversary." National Weather Service. https://www.weather.gov/ctp/ TornadoOutbreak_May311985.

2. Bistas, Karlyle, and Ramneet Grewal. 2023. "The Intricacies of Survivor's Guilt: Exploring Its Phenomenon Across Contexts." *Cureus* 15, no. 9 (September). 10.7759/ cureus.45703. 1-2

3. Substance Abuse and Mental Health Services Administration. 2023. "Warning Signs and Risk Factors for Emotional Distress." SAMHSA. https://www.samhsa.gov/find-help/disaster-distress-helpline/warning-signs-risk-factors.

4. Substance Abuse and Mental Health Services Administration. 2014. "Understanding Compassion Fatigue." SAMHSA Publications. https://store.samhsa.gov/sites/default/files/sma14-4869.pdf.

5. Ibid.

Chapter 4: The Outhouse

1. Van der Kolk, Bessel A. 2015. *The Body Keeps the Score: Brain, Mind, and Body in the Healing of Trauma*. New York, New York: Penguin Publishing Group. 226-227

2. Ulrich, Jessica Sanigaq, LaVerne Xilegg Demientieff, and Emma Elliott. 2022. "Storying and restorying: Co-creating Indigenous well-being through Relational Knowledge Exchange." *American Review of Canadian Studies* 52, no. 3 (October): 247-259. 10.1080/02722011.2022.2095498. 249

3. Ibid. 250

4. Delony, John. 2023. *Building a Non-Anxious Life*. N.p.: Ramsey Press.

Chapter 5: The Neighbors

1. Brown, Brené. 2021. *Atlas of the Heart: Mapping Meaningful Connection and the Language of Human Experience*. N.p.: Random House Publishing Group. 6

2. Birk, Jeffery. 2023. "Chronic Stress Can Hurt Your Overall Health." Columbia Doctors. https://www.columbiadoctors.org/news/chronic-stress-can-hurt-your-overall-health.

3. Sederer, Lloyd I. 2019. "What Does "Rat Park" Teach Us About Addiction?" Psychiatric Times. https://www.psychiatrictimes.com/view/what-does-rat-park-teach-us-about-addiction.

Chapter 6: The Baby

1. Brown, Brené. 2021. *Atlas of the Heart: Mapping Meaningful Connection and the Language of Human Experience.* N.p.: Random House Publishing Group. 110-111

2. Booker, Adriel. 2013. "How to help and care for a friend after miscarriage (and pregnancy loss)." Adriel Booker. https://adrielbooker.com/care-for-a-friend-after-miscarriage-or-stillbirth/.

Chapter 7: The School Assembly

1. Brown, Brené. 2021. *Atlas of the Heart: Mapping Meaningful Connection and the Language of Human Experience.* N.p.: Random House Publishing Group. 92-93

2. Demientieff, LaVerne Xilegg, and Patrick P. Frank. 2022. "I Remember Who I Am: Deg Xit'an Athabascan Perspective on Wellness." In *Indigenous Knowledge and Mental Health: A Global Perspective*, edited by David Danto and Masood Zangeneh, 213-237. N.p.: Springer International Publishing. https://doi.org/10.1007/978-3-030-71346-1_13. 214

Chapter 8: The Chad Story

1. Centers for Disease Control and Prevention. 2024. "Fentanyl Facts." Centers for Disease Control and Prevention. https://www.cdc.gov/stopoverdose/fentanyl/.

2. National Institutes of Health. 2024. "The Opioid Crisis." NIH HEAL Initiative. https://heal.nih.gov/about/opioid-crisis.

3. Ibid.

4. Centers for Disease Control and Prevention. 2024. "Fentanyl Facts." Centers for Disease Control and Prevention. https://www.cdc.gov/stopoverdose/fentanyl/.

5. Arora, Saachi, and Sangeeta Bhatia. 2023. "Addressing Grief and Bereavement in Covid-19 Pandemic." *Illness, Crisis, and Loss*, (January). 10.1177/10541373221145536.1

6. Winfrey, Oprah, and Bruce D. Perry. 2021. *What Happened to You? Conversations on Trauma, Resilience, and Healing*. N.p.: Flatiron Books. 17

Chapter 9: The Addiction

1. Clemson University Extension Service. n.d. "pH Values of Common Foods and Ingredients." pH Values of Common Foods and Ingredients. Accessed June 3, 2024. https://www.clemson.edu/extension/food/food2market/documents/ph_of_common_foods.pdf.

2. Main, Emily. 2012. "5 Great Reasons to Kick Your Soda Habit." Today.com. https://www.today.com/health/5-great-reasons-kick-your-soda-habit-398323.

3. Consumer Reports. 2014. "Caramel color in Soda may be a health risk." Consumer Reports. https://www.con-

sumerreports.org/cro/news/2014/01/caramel-color-the-health-risk-that-may-be-in-your-soda/index.htm.

4. US Food and Drug Administration. 2023. "Brominated Vegetable Oil (BVO)." US Food and Drug Administration. https://www.fda.gov/food/food-additives-petitions/brominated-vegetable-oil-bvo.

5. Ibid.

6. Bauer, Brent A. 2023. "What is BPA, and what are the concerns about BPA?" Mayo Clinic. https://www.mayoclinic.org/healthy-lifestyle/nutrition-and-healthy-eating/expert-answers/bpa/faq-20058331.

7. Harvard T.H. Chan School of Public Health. 2023. "Low-Calorie and Artificial Sweeteners – The Nutrition Source." The Nutrition Source. https://nutritionsource.hsph.harvard.edu/healthy-drinks/artificial-sweeteners/.

8. Mayo Clinic. 2022. "Caffeine: How much is too much?" Mayo Clinic. https://www.mayoclinic.org/healthy-lifestyle/nutrition-and-healthy-eating/in-depth/caffeine/art-20045678.

9. TIME Magazine. 2021. *The Science of Addiction: What We Know. What We're Learning*, Special TIME Edition. New York, NY: Meridith Corporation. 14

10. Ibid. 10

11. Muskeg Wellness. 2024. *Traditional Path for Indigenous Wellness through Peer Support*, Peer Support Training with Alaska's Indigenous Tribal Traditions. Fairbanks Native Association, Fairbanks, Alaska, USA. In-Person Training.

Chapter 10: The Ride

1. Yehuda, Rachel, and Amy Lehrner. 2018. "Intergenerational transmission of trauma effects: putative role of epigenetic mechanisms." *World Psychiatry: Official journal of the World Psychiatric Association (WPA)* 17, no. 3 (October): 243-257. https://doi.org/10.1002/wps.20568.

2. Swenson-Ridley, Alexandra. 2023. *Unearthing Selfless Syndrome: The Journey to Renewing Your Energy and Reclaiming Yourself.* 1st ed. N.p.: Dr. Alexandra Swenson-Ridley. 63-65

3. Groeschel, Craig. 2023. "3 Questions to Ask Before You Communicate." Craig Groeschel. https://www.craig-groeschel.com/blog/3-questions-to-ask-before-you-communicate.

4. Demientieff, LaVerne Xilegg, and Patrick P. Frank. 2022. "I Remember Who I am: Deg Xit'an Athabascan Perspective on Wellness." In *Indigenous Knowledge and Mental Health: A Global Perspective,* edited by David Danto and Masood Zangeneh, 213-237. N.p.: Springer International Publishing. https://doi.org/10.1007/978-3-030-71346-1_13. 223-224

REFERENCES

Arora, Saachi, and Sangeeta Bhatia. "Addressing Grief and Bereavement in Covid-19 Pandemic." *Illness, Crisis, and Loss*, Jan. 2023, doi:10.1177/10541373221145536.

Bauer, Brent A. "What Is BPA, and What Are the Concerns About BPA?" *Mayo Clinic*, 2023, www.mayoclinic.org/healthy-lifestyle/nutrition-and-healthy-eating/expert-answers/bpa/faq-20058331.

Birk, Jeffery. "Chronic Stress Can Hurt Your Overall Health." *Columbia Doctors*, 2023, www.columbiadoctors.org/news/chronic-stress-can-hurt-your-overall-health.

Bistas, Karlyle, and Ramneet Grewal. "The Intricacies of Survivor's Guilt: Exploring Its Phenomenon Across Contexts." *Cureus*, vol. 15, no. 9, Sept. 2023, doi:10.7759/cureus.45703.

Booker, Adriel. "How to Help and Care for a Friend After Miscarriage (and Pregnancy Loss)." *Adriel Booker*, 2013, www.adrielbooker.com/care-for-a-friend-after-miscarriage-or-stillbirth/.

Brown, Brené. *Atlas of the Heart: Mapping Meaningful Connection and the Language of Human Experience*. Random House Publishing Group, 2021.

Centers for Disease Control and Prevention. "Fentanyl Facts." *Centers for Disease Control and Prevention*, 2024, www.cdc.gov/stopoverdose/fentanyl/.

Clemson University Extension Service. "pH Values of Common Foods and Ingredients." *pH Values of Common Foods and Ingredients*, n.d. Accessed 3 June 2024, www.clemson.edu/extension/food/food2market/documents/ph_of_common_foods.pdf.

Consumer Reports. "Caramel Color in Soda May Be a Health Risk." *Consumer Reports*, 2014, www.consumerreports.org/cro/news/2014/01/caramel-color-the-health-risk-that-may-be-in-your-soda/index.htm.

Delony, John. *Building a Non-Anxious Life*. Ramsey Press, 2023.

Demientieff, LaVerne Xilegg, and Patrick P. Frank. "I Remember Who I Am: Deg Xit'an Athabascan Perspective on Wellness." *Indigenous Knowledge and Mental Health: A Global Perspective*, edited by David Danto and Masood Zangeneh, Springer International Publishing, 2022, pp. 213-237, doi:10.1007/978-3-030-71346-1_13.

Groeschel, Craig. "3 Questions to Ask Before You Communicate." *Craig Groeschel*, 2023, www.craiggroeschel.com/blog/3-questions-to-ask-before-you-communicate.

Harvard T.H. Chan School of Public Health. "Low-Calorie and Artificial Sweeteners – The Nutrition Source." *The*

Nutrition Source, 2023, https://nutritionsource.hsph.harvard.edu/healthy-drinks/artificial-sweeteners/.

James, Karin H., and Laura Engelhardt. "The Effects of Handwriting Experience on Functional Brain Development in Pre-Literate Children." *Trends in Neuroscience and Education*, vol. 1, no. 1, Dec. 2012, pp. 32-42, doi:10.1016/j.tine.2012.08.001.

Main, Emily. "5 Great Reasons to Kick Your Soda Habit." *Today.com*, 2012, www.today.com/health/5-great-reasons-kick-your-soda-habit-398323.

Mayo Clinic. "Caffeine: How Much Is Too Much?" *Mayo Clinic*, 2022, www.mayoclinic.org/healthy-lifestyle/nutrition-and-healthy-eating/in-depth/caffeine/art-20045678.

Muskeg Wellness. *Traditional Path for Indigenous Wellness Through Peer Support, Peer Support Training with Alaska's Indigenous Tribal Traditions*. Fairbanks Native Association, 2024. In-person training.

National Institutes of Health. "The Opioid Crisis." *NIH HEAL Initiative*, 2024, https://heal.nih.gov/about/opioid-crisis.

NeuroRelay. "How Does Writing Affect Your Brain?" *NeuroRelay*, 2013, http://neurorelay.com/2013/08/07/how-does-writing-affect-your-brain/.

Schaefer, Carol. *Grandmothers Counsel the World: Women Elders Offer Their Vision for Our Planet*. Shambhala, 2006.

Sederer, Lloyd I. "What Does 'Rat Park' Teach Us About Addiction?" *Psychiatric Times*, 2019, www.psychiatrictimes.com/view/what-does-rat-park-teach-us-about-addiction.

Sleptzoff, Nick. "Weather.gov > State College, PA > May 31, 1985 Tornado Outbreak: 35th Anniversary." *National Weather Service*, 1985, www.weather.gov/ctp/ TornadoOutbreak_May311985.

Smyth, J. M., A. A. Stone, A. Hurewitz, and A. Kaell. "Effects of Writing About Stressful Experiences on Symptom Reduction in Patients With Asthma or Rheumatoid Arthritis: A Randomized Trial." *JAMA*, vol. 281, no. 14, Apr. 1999, pp. 1304-1309, doi:10.1001/jama.281.14.1304.

Substance Abuse and Mental Health Services Administration. "Understanding Compassion Fatigue." *SAMHSA Publications*, 2014, https://store.samhsa.gov/sites/ default/files/sma14-4869.pdf.

Substance Abuse and Mental Health Services Administration. "Warning Signs and Risk Factors for Emotional Distress." *SAMHSA*, 2023, www.samhsa.gov/find-help/disaster-distress-helpline/warning-signs-risk-factors.

Swenson-Ridley, Alexandra. *Unearthing Selfless Syndrome: The Journey to Renewing Your Energy and Reclaiming Yourself.* 1st ed., Dr. Alexandra Swenson-Ridley, 2023.

TIME Magazine. The Science of Addiction: What We Know. What We're Learning, special ed., Meredith Corporation, 2021.

Ulrich, Jessica Sanigaq, LaVerne Xilegg Demientieff, and Emma Elliott. "Storying and Restorying: Co-Creating Indigenous Well-Being Through Relational Knowledge Exchange." *American Review of Canadian Studies*, vol. 52, no. 3, Oct. 2022, pp. 247-259, doi:10.1080/02722011.2022.2 095498.

US Department of Transportation National Highway Traffic Safety Administration. "Drunk Driving | Statistics and Resources." *NHTSA*, 2023, www.nhtsa.gov/risky-driving/drunk-driving.

US Food and Drug Administration. "Brominated Vegetable Oil (BVO)." *US Food and Drug Administration*, 2023, www.fda.gov/food/food-additives-petitions/brominated-vegetable-oil-bvo.

Van der Kolk, Bessel A. *The Body Keeps the Score: Brain, Mind, and Body in the Healing of Trauma.* Penguin Publishing Group, 2015.

Van der Weel, F. R., and Audrey L. Van der Meer. "Handwriting but Not Typewriting Leads to Widespread Brain Connectivity: A High-Density EEG Study with Implications for the Classroom." *Frontiers in Psychology*, vol. 14, no. 2023, Jan. 2024, doi:10.3389/fpsyg.2023.1219945.

Winfrey, Oprah, and Bruce D. Perry. *What Happened to You? Conversations on Trauma, Resilience, and Healing.* Flatiron Books, 2021.

Yehuda, Rachel, and Amy Lehrner. "Intergenerational Transmission of Trauma Effects: Putative Role of Epigenetic Mechanisms." *World Psychiatry: Official Journal of the World Psychiatric Association (WPA)*, vol. 17, no. 3, Oct. 2018, pp. 243-257, doi:10.1002/wps.20568.

MASTER RESOURCE LIST

Resources are provided at the end of each chapter, but all of them have been compiled here with the hopes that if you need them in the future, it will be easy for you to locate.

Crisis?

Please call or text 988 to talk to someone

General Information Resource for most topics covered

SAMHSA (Substance Abuse and Mental Health Services Administration. https://www.samhsa.gov/find-help/national-helpline or 1-800-662-4357

Reach out to your healthcare provider

Alcohol

AA (Alcoholics Anonymous) https://www.aa.org/

The National Institute on Aging https://www.nia.nih.gov/health/how-help-someone-you-know-who-drinks-too-much

Veterans

https://www.maketheconnection.net/conditions/alcohol-use-disorder

https://www.maketheconnection.net/resources/self-help

Disasters

Disaster Distress Helpline at 1-800-985-5990 or www.disasterdistress.samhsa.gov.

A general informational resource is SAMHSA (Substance Abuse and Mental Health Services Administration. https://www.samhsa.gov/find-help/national-helpline or 1-800-662-4357

Mental Health

The National Council for Mental Wellbeing https://www.thenationalcouncil.org/

NAMI (National Alliance on Mental Illness) Helpline is 1-800-950-6264. You can also find resources and support at https://www.nami.org/

National Institute of Mental Health offers research and resources at https://www.nimh.nih.gov/

Mental Health First Aid Training https://www.mentalhealthfirstaid.org/

Demientieff, L.X., Frank, P. (2022). *I Remember Who I Am: Deg Xit'an Athabascan Perspectives on Wellness. In: Danto, D., Zangeneh, M. (eds) Indigenous Knowledge and Mental Health*. Springer, Cham. https://doi.org/10.1007/978-3-030-71346-1_13

NAMI (National Alliance on Mental Illness) Helpline is 1-800-950-6264. You can also find resources and support at https://www.nami.org/

Miscarriage

Information on the different types of miscarriages and the help you may need: https://www.tommys.org/baby-loss-support/miscarriage-information-and-support/types-of-miscarriage

Adriel Booker, whose book *Grace Like Scarlett: Grieving Hope after Miscarriage and Loss,* offers a community support group, Our Scarlett Stories. You can find her story and resources at https://adrielbooker.com/grace-like-scarlett/.

Author Diane Newcomer has a website that addresses topics like infertility, miscarriage, grief, and suffering. You can find her at https://dianenewcomer.com/.

Suggestions of things to do after having a miscarriage: https://www.nct.org.uk/pregnancy/miscarriage/miscarriage-eight-things-can-help-afterwards

Author Jenny Albers wrote *Courageously Expecting,* addressing pregnancy after loss, and can be found here: https://jennyalbers.com/courageously-expecting/

Dr. Rachelle Keng addresses the anxiety that can surround a woman during and right after pregnancy in her book *Woven in the Womb*. You can order her book and find resources at https://www.rachellekeng.com/.

Opioid/Addictions

The National Institute of Health has the HEAL project, where you can find information on the Opioid Crisis: https://heal.nih.gov/

Information on HALT, a helpful technique for identifying triggers that lead to addictive behaviors: https://bradfordhealth.com/halt-hunger-anger-loneliness-tiredness/

Grief

Dealing with grief, especially with children: https://good-grief.org/resources/

An overall resource: https://optionb.org/

Books

The Body Keeps the Score: Brain, Mind, and Body in the Healing of Trauma by Bessel van der Kolk

Winning the War of your Mind: Change Your Thinking, Change Your Life by Craig Groeschel

Building a Non-Anxious Life by Dr. John Delony

Own Your Past Change Your Future by Dr. John Delony

Atlas of the Heart by Dr. Brené Brown